Honoring Your Parents

One man's journey as viewed
through the lens of the Bible

Gayle Jackson

PRESS

Prologue

This book is written to teach children, of all ages, the truths concerning the gravity, issues, pains and pitfalls experienced in honoring their parents. It is written to parents to make them aware of the issue so they will teach their children to honor them. It is written from my perspective of our parents' aging process. It concerns itself with the response of children and the parents.

We must realize that honoring was the single most important familial command in the Ten Commandments and was emphasized by Jesus. It is one of the keys for a healthy society. All strong societies are built on strong families, and a vital ingredient to a strong family is the honoring of parents.

My mother and my wife's mother lived with us during their aging years. This odyssey covered eighteen years of our life. This book is a compilation of my observations and studies done over those eighteen years, as I viewed this journey through the lens of my truth system, the Bible.

The book contains my observations and applications from my personal journal. This is not an exhaustive work or writings from a research project on honoring parents. The major observations are annotated and are called "Lessons." They are documented in the context of the book and are restated in the appendix.

I assure you this entire journey was a struggle. I had little, if any, victories or revelations that "solved the problem" of aging parents because the problem could not be solved. It was a struggle because of the lack of answers and positive feedback. I was to serve and not fix.

Though I am a professing Christian, this book is intended for all people who desire to learn about and gain some insights into the Honoring your Parents principles. My story is not an unusual one; rather it is a typical story for many families. If you haven't already, you will face the aging parent issue. This problem cannot be solved by national legislation; it must be mitigated one family at a time. I encourage you to take a deep breath and plan on this approaching phase of your life.

I have spoken on this subject many times in different venues. I realized there is a real need in the marketplace for information on how to treat and live with an aging parent. As I began to convert my thoughts to paper, I realized the difficulty of putting a talk into a book. Bear with me as I try to convey thoughts and feelings to you about this issue, both as a topic and as a life story.

Note: I had a person preview this book and he was disturbed because he thought it reflected no hope in the aging parent circumstance. Let me state that while the end of the story is death, the family's hope is in their chance to fulfill the life cycle and love their parents to the end. It is a great gift to love the parents as they exit the earth. Since aging will be our future also, we should participate in the process with joy.

This book is dedicated to the memory of Mary Marguerite Jackson and Eva Lou Sisco.

Table Of Contents

A study of Jesus' last moments on the earth gives us an insight into His view of this earthly responsibility. Biblical examples of honoring, such as Jesus' time on the cross, bring into focus the importance of this command to God.

This chapter reviews the biblical command from the Old Testament and New Testament writings, and the meaning of the word "honor." The commands are traced from the Ten Commandments (the Decalogue) to the teachings of Jesus and Paul. These insights reveal the gravity and importance God places in honoring our parents.

The command of honoring has different applications at different stages of our life. The truth of "Honor Your Parents" never changes, but the application changes. The way we looked at our parents when we were teenagers differs from our 40-year-old observation. True honoring requires that we understand this evolution of perspective.

This chapter reviews my experiences and the experiences of others in dealing with the aging parent problem. There are applications from all of the different positions and observations.

Death is where the journey of "Honoring Your Parents" ends and your story as the aging parent begins. This chapter discusses the biblical perspective of death.

Discussion guide available at www.Honorurparents.com
Books may be ordered at the same web site or
WisdomHunters.com

Introduction

I was raised on the high plains of Texas during the WWII years. I had the fortune of having a good mother and dad who were committed to the family and our upbringing. My parents had been raised in a small town in Arkansas and also had a stable family history. We were simple people who had a love of family, country and God. During my journey as a child, I witnessed my grandparents care for their 90-year-old paternal mother in their home. I also watched my parents deal with their aging parents with love and respect and sacrificial care. It was an honest model of struggle, resolve and suffering. Even with this great modeling, when it came my time to help, I struggled with the concept.

My parents' lives had spanned two World Wars and the Great Depression, and in their life they lost their first child. Despite these difficulties, the concept of "taking care of our own" prevailed. The care and nurturing of the family was always of high importance. As I have gotten older, I have gained enormous respect for their courage and character in surviving and prospering during those years. Sometimes it takes elapsed years to appreciate the accomplishments of your parents.

During all of those times of trial, they never abandoned their parents. My mother's father died young, and her mother was not one to be alone. So Mother and Dad moved her in with them when she was in her fifties. Our house was large for the time; it was probably 1800 square feet, with three bedrooms and one bathroom (note please *one* bathroom!) It housed Mother and Dad, my grandmother and my brother and me. My grandmother stayed thirty years. Therefore, Mother and Dad had little to no time by themselves in their journey through life. It was rough having two "mothers" in the house, and it created problems at times; however, my parents faithfully continued to care for her. Dad died before my grandmother died; he was always concerned she would outlive him and she did.

I married Connie Sisco when we were both in our early twenties and we began our new family life. Connie's father died the day we were to be married and my dad died three years later, so both my mother and Connie's mother were widowed early in our marriage and were left to our care during their transition years of growing older. Connie and I both had a sibling with whom we had to work out the strategies and details of our mothers' care. Each sibling's family had a totally different relational dynamic than ours. This created stress between us, our siblings, and our mothers. Each sibling also lived in a different city than our own. There were struggles and we stumbled through these times. Chapter 4 addresses these issues in greater detail.

At the age of 70 my mother began to show a slippage mentally and by the time she was 75, she had lost her mental faculties. She was a victim of acute senile dementia. She became incapacitated, incontinent and erratic in her behavior. But even when lost in the darkness of a destroyed mind, she remained loving. Eventually we put her in a home for her care. She died there of a stroke six months later.

On the other hand, Eva, Connie's mother, had a sharp mind until she was 87. Due to many factors, she had only modest means to handle her financial needs and lived with us for 12 years. Eva was a sweet and caring person who never complained about the circumstances of getting older. The last five years of her life, she became nearly blind and very hard of hearing. Connie remembers the sadness of realizing her mother could no longer hear the birds sing. Eva loved colors and beautiful things and to read large print books. All of these interests she lost to blindness.

As life went on Eva was in constant pain and discomfort. Yet she lived her life to the fullest that she could and never griped. She continued to enjoy the Dallas Cowboys and the Atlanta Braves. It wasn't until her oldest daughter Jane passed away that the loss seemed to take the fight out of Eva, and she died.

Our mothers were very different people with their own styles, but both were gracious and good to have around. They both had lived through tough years. I learned a lot from them during their aging process. Though the journey at times was not pretty, the mothers taught me much about courage, service, attitude, and love. They were noble in their handling of the rough times they had in living and aging. Now as I get older, I better realize the depth of their achievement: they never complained and were grateful to the end. I am sure I got more out of them than they did out of me.

Lesson 1: As the parent, a good attitude and gratitude about the state of affairs is mandatory for good relations with the caregiver. The parent's gratitude may be a reflection of how much you are grateful for them.

I introduce you to the two mothers so they will be real to you. They are not the object of a clinical study, but are merely two humans who experienced the good and bad of life.

Chapter 1

The Biblical Example of Honoring

John 19:25

"Now there stood by the Cross of Jesus His mother, and His mother's sister, Mary the wife of Clopas, and Mary Magdalene.

19:26

When Jesus therefore saw His mother, and the disciple whom He loved standing by, He said to His mother, "Woman, behold your son!"

19:27

Then He said to the disciple, "Behold your mother!" And from that hour that disciple took her to his own home.

19:28

After this, Jesus, knowing that all things were now accomplished, that the Scripture might be fulfilled"

These verses contain comments made by Jesus during His time on the cross. Let's notice some things about this scene. To set the stage, Jesus' crucifixion is the climatic moment in God's plan for the rescue of mankind. Biblically speaking, it is the time all God's events pointed to after the incident of the fall of man in the Garden of Eden. It had been prophesized time and again throughout the Old Testament.[1] It was alluded to in Genesis.[2] The dilemma of man is his separation from God; this dilemma is not unique to the Christian faith, but is a problem in all religions and mythology. The cross was God's answer to man's dilemma. The issue of sin and separation from God began with the disobedience of Adam and Eve. It was now being reconciled on the cross with Jesus' sacrifice. During His time on the cross before His death, Jesus said little, but what He said is of utmost importance.

Let us focus on what the apostle John records while observing Christ on the cross. John 19:26-27 documents the last comments Jesus makes on earthly matters. Jesus, knowing He was dying, takes His "honoring your parent" responsibility for Mary and passes it on to John. In the midst of His suffering Jesus took time to look after his mother: He assigned her care to one of His disciples. Not only was His sacrificial work on the cross sufficient to save all of mankind, but He modeled obedience to the command "honor your parents."

Notice, Jesus did not pass the job of honoring on to one of His blood brothers; rather it was to His disciple, John. In musing about Jesus' decision to give the role to a disciple and not a sibling, I studied the Bible on sibling relationships. In reviewing the job descriptions for different relationships, such as spouse, boss, employee, friend, enemy, and citizen, there was a significant absence of a definition of a sibling relationship in the New Testament. There are Old Testament lessons alluding to these relationships[3] but no direct job description or special instructions for a sibling relationship. This doesn't mean it is not an important relationship in our life; but it does mean the sibling relationship in the New

Testament is nothing more than a relationship with another person.

Jesus says, "….who are my brothers and my mother…"[4] He declares His spiritual brothers are His family. We tend to put great weight on the sibling relationship but in the order of Christian relationships, there does not appear to be any special emphasis placed on the sibling relationship. It appears spiritual brotherhood is the more important relationship. The lesson of honoring is a special spiritual assignment and duty from God.

Just before my dad died, he told Mother to look to their sons. There was an assignment of responsibility. It was a passing on of the honoring role for our mother. Dad's thinking was one of pride and a reflection of what he had learned from his father. He felt he had raised two boys to honor and take care of his wife, our mother. Though my brother and I were untrained and ill prepared, we still had a job to do. In retrospect, I now know we needed help.

Lesson 2: With all the complexity of retirements, estates and taxes, you will need all the experts you can get.

Also note that when Jesus was finished with the job assignment for John, He said, "Knowing that all things were now **accomplished**"[5] Jesus "gave up the ghost."[6] Apparently, things were not finished until His mother was taken care of. Jesus says earlier in the Garden of Gethsemane, "It is finished" in reference to the preparing of the disciples. During the total cross experience Jesus says, "It is finished"[7] twice. Therefore, it appears Jesus had three jobs to finish before His death: His preparation of the disciples, dying for mankind, and the assignment of honoring His mother. All were done.

This scene at the cross is a dramatic illustration of the importance God places on honoring parents. Think about it:

Jesus could have made this reassignment of His mother's care and honor at the last supper, on the way down the road, or in secret with John, but no; He took time on the cross to make His honoring commitment known and recorded for all.

This event is overwhelming evidence of the importance God places on honoring parents. I think it could be said that as we honor our parents, we are modeling the cross-bearing commitment for our children. With such weight as the example of Jesus, one must ask, "How then ought we to live?"

Chapter 2

The Commandment(s)

Section 1: The Command, from the Decalogue

Deuteronomy 5:16 *"Honor your father and your mother, as the Lord your God has commanded you, that your days may be long and that it may be well with you in the land which the Lord your God is giving you."*

When the Israelites were freed from slavery and came out of Egypt, they crossed the desert to a place known as Mt. Sinai. Here God gave Moses His laws and precepts required to have a working society and nation. Remember the Israelites had been a nation of slaves for hundreds of years; they were tribal in government, and never had to rule nationally for themselves. Though they had social mores of conduct, some cultural and some Egyptian, they had not heard from their God on how to conduct the affairs of a society. They were a people without a legal or national social system. The commands given at Sinai were the basis on which to build a society and that society exists even today, some 4,000 years later. This feat has not been repeated by any societal group anytime in history.

As the Jews began this relationship with God, they had to realize all the commands from God were in their best interest; they were not just prohibitions and they were not just suggestions. They were precepts designed in the best interest of the people and the society and were to be obeyed. If the people did not embrace this view about the Law, they would begin to drift into disobedience and idolatry for their comfort and convenience sake. Over history, societies without these truths at their core or societies which ignored these truths have gone into chaos, lost world status, fell into depravation and ultimately dissolved.

The Ten Commandments are a body of law from which a number of legal systems have been formed. Not until just recently, in our modern society, are these precepts of God taking a back seat to worldly conjectures. It will be interesting to see what repercussions this brings over the next century.

One of the first groups of commands God gave the new nation of Israel was the Decalogue. Ten commands would be the cornerstone of all behavior within their nation. These commands would be the key to a healthy society and future stability.

Exodus 20:12 *"Honor your father and your mother, that your days may be long upon the land which the Lord your God is giving you."*

When we study the Decalogue, we notice six of the commands (5 through 10) are societal laws governing behavior on the temporal level. The second of these six commandments is "Honor your Parents," and is the only one dealing with the family. We can deduce a Biblical key to community health is found in the society's view of parents and how children deal with parents. From historical experience, we may also conclude three axioms:

First, honoring your parents is not intuitively natural, and we need a law to bring us into line;

Second, all people need protection when they no longer can contribute to the well-being of a family or society or themselves; and **Third,** a society that demeans and rejects parents is a society out of step with God.

Note that "Honor your father and your mother..." is the only command in the Decalogue to have an attendant promise: **"that your days may be long upon the land which the Lord your God is giving you."** Let me suggest the promise is there because honoring your parents can be so tough to obey and execute, we need motivation.

Lesson 3: We always do things we perceive are worthwhile and in our best interest. Altruism is by in large a myth.

Lesson 4: To stay obedient to the commands, we must believe there is temporal and eternal value for us in obedience.

We can dishonor our parents and not sense or understand the negative result in the short term. The parents' response to our conduct will not reflect the quality of our "honoring" behavior. The feedback is within ourselves and found in our confidence that we have been doing what is right and commanded. Remember for your sanity and attitude, the quality of your effort will not be measured by your parental response.

I had always thought honoring meant to obey my parents and to say, Yes ma'am" and "no sir", etc. My appreciation and application of the command broke down as I got older and our relationship became more complex. As an illustration, the way I saw Mother when I was a teenager was no longer valid when I was a middle-aged man. This observation may seem apparent to the reader, but I was surprised when I discovered this truth. The relationship between Mother and me needed to change and no matter how much I hated it, I had to change. I realize now that we all desire to freeze-frame parts of our life and keep the sweet memory, but that is not possible in the complex relationship of parent/child.

In retrospect I realized the relationship had changed numerous times, but I had not changed with it. I think Mother had adjusted, but I had not. As I am now older, I think I see the same miscalculation with my children. Later, as she slid into her reduced mental capacity, there was no way I could consider obeying her. How could I obey one who had diminished mental capabilities? This was hard, even shocking to me, since I had not given my view of honoring any thought for over twenty years. When Mother began to slip, I knew I had an unworkable definition of honoring and had better understand the command and our relationship before I went forward.

Lesson 5: Remember, no one in heaven will say they are glad they did not do what God commanded. No one will ultimately say they are glad they did not honor their parents.

Section 2: The Promise

Deuteronomy 5:16 *"Honor your father and your mother, as the Lord your God has commanded you, that your days may be long and that it may be well with you in the land which the Lord your God is giving you."*

It is a difficult thing to hear people lament about their relationship with their parents. I have witnessed this distress numerous times and recommend we do all within our power to avoid it. The unsaid things, the harsh comments, ignoring or manipulating each other, not liking them, etc. will come back to haunt us. I have known people who have broken a relationship with their parents later in life as the relationship got too hard or too inconvenient. All of these couples experienced unrest and disruption in their lives as the years went on. The ones who broke the relationship missed the promise and are damaged. They had forgotten it is mentally, emotionally and spiritually important for their parents to finish the last chapter of their lives being honored.

In today's society there is feel-good advice on relationships. If the relationship does not feed you emotionally, you have no obligation or need or reason to put up with it. Get rid of the relationship, society says. Discard it and move on. This advice is counter-scriptural to the command on honoring you parents. Do not fall prey to such inane thinking as to disregard the honor command. Remember

Lesson 6: *The promise associated with honoring your parent is not that you would feel good during the experience, but rather it would go well with you all your days.*

To obey this command brought a reward for *"days to be long"* and also *"it will be well with you."* What the phrases "days to be long" and "be well with you" might be are hard to define, but God is saying special favor rests on the one who honors his parents. We do not need the details of what the reward will look like. We need to trust in the promise of God. It has got to be good. And the negative side of the promise is enough to sober one up.

We operate this way all the time with our children. We teach them good hygiene, nutrition, manners, etc. so it will go well with them. None of these disciplines have an immediate feedback but are proven concepts to a good life.

I have wondered what this promise could mean: *"it may be well with you in the land which the Lord your God is giving you."* In trying to explain this promise to my children, I told them it was to have peace in my life concerning the chapter of my aging parent(s). Peace is an illusive quality, especially as we get older. Older people tend to live with regret. To have peace about our past is a treasure. To have peace concerning our parental relationship is a positive stroke for anyone.

To be *"well with you in the land"* is saying the family heritage is better because of obedience to the command.

One of my concerns was staying motivated in this journey with the aging parents. Motivation is a key to all we do. Do not underestimate the need for the correct motivation when living life and honoring your parents. I think this is why God gave us the promise.

Over the eight years of mother's infirmity, my love for her kept me motivated to hang in there with her over the long run. But in dealing with my mother, I realized the promise for the future kept me motivated day-to-day and event-to-event. When I bathed her, stayed with her during the night, cleaned up her mess, fed her, put ointment on her bedsores or cut her toenails, the thought of the promise kept me going. The promise always motivated me back into the battle.

In reviewing history, we can observe that as most societies developed and prospered and as these prospering societies aged into the third and fourth generation, parental abuse increased. I am not sure of the cause and effect of this observation but there is a correlation. It appears the more prosperity, the more abuse. When reviewing our present age, we note parents being abandoned at an alarming rate. This is a catalyst for euthanasia. Though the quality of life argument is the one most often used for euthanasia, it seems to me that euthanasia becomes an acceptable option when the personal inconvenience or expense factor of the aging parent becomes dominant. With increased government spending on the aged, such as Social Security and Medicare, the thinking may become that it is advisable to allow euthanasia in order to lower our expenditures as a society. How frightening!

In *Undaunted Courage* by Steven Ambrose, the author noted when the aging Indian parents could no longer contribute to getting food or protecting the tribe, they were forcefully abandoned to die outside the camp. Is this where we are headed today?

As I get older, a truth I have observed is old age kills most temporal hope. Each day the world system reinforces to the elderly the concept they are not needed any more. The elderly are tolerated more than revered or appreciated. They are becoming irrelevant. I was guilty of this attitude towards my grandmother when I was younger and as I enter my elder years, I am aware of the problem of becoming personally obsolete.

The answer to the dilemma of honoring the aging parent is not found in governmental or retirement programs, but in the attitude and relationship of the families in our society. And we will honor during this difficult time as we are motivated. As noted earlier, this motivation is found in the promise attached to the command of children honoring their parents. Though I receive Social Security, I wonder if this entitlement has dulled our sense of responsibility to our parents.

Three of the best things you can do for your children are to love God, love your spouse and honor your parents.

Section 3: What Does the Word Honor Mean?

In the New Testament to honor your parent means
   1. to estimate, fix the value
       a. for the value of something belonging to one's self
   2. to revere, venerate[2]

The Oxford English Dictionary defines it as:

1. High respect, esteem, reverence, accorded to exalted worth or rank, deferential admiration or approbation, as felt or entertained in the mind for some person or thing
2. Exalted rank or position; dignity, distinction
3. Something conferred or done as a token of respect or distinction; a mark or manifestation of high regard; a position or title of rank, a degree of nobility, a dignity

Honoring your parents by these definitions lead us to the truth

Lesson 7: Your parents' value is not determined by their performance in your relationship. Their value is determined by your ascribing value to them.

Rather, you as the child must attribute value to the parents. Honoring is the act of conferring value to your parents. The commandment instructs you to value your parents irrespective of their performance. Remember, you value your parents because you declare they are of value, not because of their responses and their track record. This assignment of value is to shape your attitude towards them.

In every society, there are abused children who dislike and distrust their parents. Being abused by a parent will create a strong force against honoring. But the Bible makes no room for this misfortune. (This is discussed more in the Appendix called "Abusive Parent.") There is no caveat or condition justifying not honoring and ascribing value to your parents. This attitude drives your performance; the performance does not drive the attitude.

The Bible says, "Honor Your Parents." We may find this repugnant or difficult, but obedience to the command is better for you and society than disobedience. Do not discard the command in your anger. Though it may be tough, the power of the Holy Spirit can make obedience possible. The truth is God is good in all things that come into our lives; refusing to honor calls into question the goodness of God and His wisdom in giving your parents to you. You must trust God, forgive your parents and obey the command.

Lesson 6*: Forgiveness does not minimize the wrong doing; forgiveness and trust in God are keys to all relationships.*

We will tend to ask God to heal our relationship with our parents. It is interesting to note that nowhere in the entire Bible did God heal a parental relationship. It appears to me the answer lies in our willingness to obey the Scriptures: forgive, make peace, serve, be willing to turn the other cheek and mentally assign your parents value. Could it be that a healed relationship is not outward happiness but inward peace, emphasizing forgiveness, and service?

"Honor Your Parents" instruct us to assign value to our parents irrespective of their behavior or their history or character. The value comes from the declaration. The least you may say about your parents is, "These are the parents God has given to me and I know they are of value in God's plan." This observation alone is sufficient to act in an honorable way towards our parents..

Section 4: Other Commands on Parent/Child

Exodus 21:17 *"And he who curses his father and his mother shall surely be put to death."*

This verse is tucked away among other verses that condemn offenders to death for transactions against other people. Since the word honor encompasses ascribing value to parents and their position, to curse would be to take the relationship to a point of complete devaluing. Disdain for the parents was not permitted in the Bible and the boys who disobeyed their parents were to be taken out of the camp and stoned. This would clearly solve a lot of teenage problems!

The Bible rarely defines both the positive and negative promises and their repercussions. But it is spelled out in the parent/child relationship. We see a major spiritual emphasis on the honor relationship of children to parents in the society. When God set up the original society, he made the honor of the parent as a cornerstone. It would do us well to pay attention.

Section 5: Jesus Comments on Honoring

Jesus, in Matthew 15:2-9, condemns twice on honoring parents.

Then the scribes and Pharisees who were from Jerusalem came to Jesus, saying, 2 "Why do your disciples transgress the tradition of the elders? For they do not wash their hands when they eat bread."[3]

3 He answered and said to them, "Why do you also transgress the commandment of God because of your tradition? 4 for God commanded, saying,

'Honor your father and your mother;' and, 'He who curses father or mother, let him be put to death.' 5 But you say,
'Whoever says to his father or mother, "Whatever profit you might have received from me is a gift to God"(Corban)— 6 then he need not honor his father or mother.' Thus you have made the commandment of God of no effect by your tradition. 7 Hypocrites! Well did Isaiah prophesy about you, saying: 8 'These people draw near to Me with their mouth,
And honor Me with their lips, but their heart is far from Me. 9 And in vain they worship Me, teaching as doctrines the commandments of men. "

Jesus is confronting the Scribes and the Pharisees on the difference between tradition and a command. The Pharisees ask Jesus: *"Why do your disciples transgress the tradition of the elders? For they do not wash their hands when they eat bread."* Note the Pharisees are focusing on the tradition of washing one's hands before eating. Jesus is affronted by their emphasizing tradition at the expense of the command to honor the parents. Jesus does not respond to their slur; rather He asks why they are in direct disobedience to the Scriptures of honoring their parents. The Pharisees had put the tradition called Corban in place of honoring their parents and had ignored the Word of God.

What was Corban? Corban was a tradition approved by the Pharisees that excused a person from providing for his parents' material needs by giving money to the temple. For example: What if I have ten dollars to give to either my parents or the temple? I am under obligation to tithe the ten dollars but I also need ten dollars to provide for my parents. The tradition of Corban says I can take my ten dollars to the temple, hand it to the priest while saying Corban, and I am excused from my obligation to support my parents.

As the Pictorial Bible Dictionary says, "That by telling the parents that their money was dedicated to God, it would be wrong to divert it from this sacred purpose... Ideally, the money thereafter belonged to God, but actually the one who made the vow might keep it in his possession." [4]Jesus took great umbrage at this tradition as it was abusive and in direct opposition to the Law of God.

Interestingly, the Scribes and Pharisees were willing to hold Jesus accountable for not washing his hands but were not willing to hold individuals responsible for their parents. Clean hands were elevated over the needs of parents and the instruction of the Decalogue. The Pharisees had devised a tradition to circumvent God's command, putting parents at risk, because of a love of money.

Lesson 8: History shows us that money can be the bane of relationships.

Before you sneer at the Pharisees, think about your own forms of Corban. You may be protecting your own quality of life or your time to live; you may be more concerned with your children's entertainment, your social commitments or the fact that your spouse doesn't like your parents, and so you are unwilling to help your parents, share with them, or care for your parents.

Again Jesus says:

Matthew 15:4 *"For God commanded, saying, "Honor your father and your Mother;" and "He who curses father or mother, let him be put to death."*

Notice Jesus packages the two commands out of the Old Testament. This should make it a special declaration. The Bible holds nothing back. This is important and if you violate it you can expect to be put to death. If not in this life, then surely there would be a negative effect in the life to come.

Section 6: Paul Comments on Honoring

Ephesians 6:2-3 *"Honor your father and mother, which is the first commandment with promise....That it may go well with you and you may live long on the earth."*

Paul repeats the Decalogue and editorializes it with **"the first commandment with a promise."** We have already discussed the promise. But consider how many commands have a promise attached? The answer is very few. Do you motivate your children with a promise when giving them a command?

Lesson 9: Not only do we need to honor our parents but also teach our children to honor us.

Section 7: Some Proverbs Concerning Parents

Pr 1:8, 6:20
*My son, hear the instruction of thy **father**, and forsake not the law of thy mother:*

Pr 13:1
*A wise son hears his **father's** instruction:*

Pr 15:5
*A fool despise his **father's** instruction:*

Pr 19:26

*He that waste his **father**, and chase away his mother,*
is a son that cause shame, and bring reproach.

Pr 20:20

*Whoso curse his **father** or his mother, his lamp shall*
be put out in obscure darkness.

Pr 23:22

*Hearken unto thy **father** that begat thee, and despise*
not thy mother when she is old.

Pr 28:24

*Who so robs his **father** or his mother, and says, It*
is no transgression; the same is the companion of a
destroyer

Pr 30:11

*There is a generation that curse their **father**, and*
doth not bless their mother.

Pr 30:17

*The eye that mocks at his **father**, and despises to obey*
his mother, the ravens of the valley shall pick it out,
and the young eagles shall eat it.

The pages of the Bible are rife with sayings concerning
parents. Read some of the attached sayings and Jewish
writings on parents in the appendix. Dishonoring parents is
a problem that has been with us for many years. It would
do us well to study the Scriptures and society and discuss
learning from past mistakes in our endeavor to be careful in
the relationship with our parents.

Section 8: Other Comments

John 5:23 *"That all men should **honor** the Son, even as they **honor** the Father. He that **honored** not the Son **honored** not the Father which hath sent him."*

To honor the Son, we must <u>obey</u> the Son. Jesus' commands are pivotal to the belief we have in Him and to our relation with Him. To disobey Jesus would mean not honoring the Son and thus dishonoring God the Father. As believers, this is not a position we want to be in.[5]

Is the command important to God? The answer is a resounding yes. We need to spend time thinking on how we may honor, not how we can get out of the command, i.e. Corban.

In review, some observations about the honor command:

a. The command is unidirectional. You are to honor your parents but your parents have no corresponding command to respond in any specific way.

b. The command is not conditional. If your parents misbehave now, it has no effect upon your responsibility to honor.

c. Additionally, your history with your parents does not excuse you from ignoring this command.

d. The consequence of disobedience to this commandment is grave, but obedience has a promised benefit.

e. The word honor means to ascribe value. That attitude shapes and drives your behavior.

f. Jesus repeated it, reprimanded the leaders for disobeying it and modeled it for us.

g. Paul repeated it.

In conclusion, it is apparent we need to learn how to obey this commandment. It has measured impact on us in our lives today and consequences for us later. It will impact our society and culture.

Chapter 3

The Metamorphosis of Honor

Introduction

As my mother passed from being a mother to a grand-mother and into the darkness of senility, I realized my relationship with her was changing: the way I related to her, the way I perceived her, the way I treated her, the way I supported her and the way I loved her. Our relationship shifted over time; therefore it stood to reason the concept of honoring her would also change. As I thought on this, I realized at different ages I needed to show different kinds of attitudes and behaviors that honored my parents (much like they, the parents, needed to show me different kinds of parenting personas.) Some of these different relationships were brought on by age and circumstance. I realized as I changed my attitudes and behavior toward Mother, I also needed to change my attitude toward my children because I was now the aging parent and they were the maturing children.

Lesson 10: In each phase of our life, our relationships to our parents change and the honoring manifestation changes with it.

Again, What does Honor mean: As discussed in Chapter 2, honoring means to ascribe or confer value to." It is not a how to word, but rather it describes the required foundational attitude needed for deciding what to do. It is a word telling us to ascribe value to our parents and this value is not dependent on their behavior, responses or history. It is a command with a unilateral responsibility, with no reciprocal response required from the parent. In other words, we must realize our parents are from God and therefore they have value. It doesn't mean we might not hurt or be angry with the history of our family; the conclusion is that the mindset must be to ascribe or confer value to them. What that might look like for you in particular I do not know, but you are responsible for figuring it out.

Lesson 11: The truth of a command stands the test of all circumstances and cultures.

One of the basic mistakes we make in studying the commands of the Bible is we consider the application of a biblical truth equal to the truth itself. Remember, truth does not change but applications do. Also, application of many commands is left to the discretion of the individual and is a product of circumstance and culture, i.e. "husbands love your wives as Christ also loved the Church and gave himself for her".[6]

However, applications of commandments stated in a negative way are not at the discretion of the individual. The command "don't steal" means "don't steal." On the other hand, "honor your parents" will look differently at different times for different people and is at the discretion of the child. As an example, we learned obeying our parents early in our life is a manifestation of honoring. There are many different changes in application with time, but the commandment "honor your parents" never varies.

In the struggle of day-to-day living, we begin to think our application is the truth. Some might say obeying your parents is the definition of honor. It may be an expression of honor but is not the definition.

Allowing application to become truth is damaging when applied to all commands, but is especially harmful in the honoring parents command. We need to teach our children to shift the honoring command from obedience when they are younger to discernment as we age. Illustration 5, page 48 depicts the different applications for the command of honoring that are required at different times of our life.

It is my observation that if children do not learn to honor during the early phases of their lives, they will have difficulty in being able to do so later. For example, if they don't obey in their youth, they will have trouble caring for the aging parent.

Lesson 12: If children do not have application for honoring their parents in their youth, they will most likely not understand the command to honor in their later years.

In my case, I witnessed Mother and Dad take my grandmother into their home for 30 years and my paternal grandfather take his mother in for a decade or more. Connie saw her mother live close to and watch over her aging parents for years. These were all significant examples of what honoring could look like. Does all honoring look like this? No. Since it is true that the application changes but the command does not, we must conclude there are other ways to honor your parents.

Lesson 13: Honoring is an action driven by an attitude and shaped by circumstance.

Taking your parent into your own home may or may not be the correct thing for you to do. The decision is predicated on circumstances, history and other factors. The decision might be a nursing home, a sibling's home, or the home of the parent's sibling. There are many manifestations but only one command.

Lesson 14: The good news is you get to determine what your "honoring" looks like, and the bad news is you must explain your conclusions to God.

In an attempt to explain and understand the thought of the metamorphosis of honoring your parent, I drew a diagram to portray the relationship of parent/child honoring. This is Illustration 5, page 48. As I tried to apply the Scriptures concerning honoring to my own life, this diagram of five phases came to me. You may see it as more or fewer phases in your life, but these five were the ones I discerned from my life. The truth is, honoring goes through multiple expressions in our lives.

Let's discuss Illustrations 1-5. Review the illustrations as you read through the accompanying explanation of each phase. In the diagram, the parent's response is from the inside going out, so the arrow points out. The child's response is from the outside going in, so the arrow points in. When the arrow points out, the word dot hatched is the response required of the parent. When the arrow points in, the word cross hatched is the response required of the child. The highlighted word and script on the outside of the pentagon are the attitudes required of the child. This diagram is a pictorial review of the changing interaction with my parents and is meant as a guideline for your thinking. You may have your own pentagon for you and your children.

Phase 1: Ages 0-13- Honor Defined by Dependence- Illustration 1

The first phase is the period of childhood. During this phase the child is totally dependent upon care and feeding from its parents. The child's honoring is demonstrated in its dependence. Remember, honoring means ascribing value to. Therefore the child shows his "ascribed value" of honor by trusting the parents and being dependent upon them. The relationship is one way because the child has no capacity to carry on any complex relationship. Therefore the relationship arrow points from the parents to the child. If the child does something harmful to the relationship, the parents must decide on the appropriate consequence which could include discipline, forgiveness and always restoration of the relationship. The child depends on the parents' care.

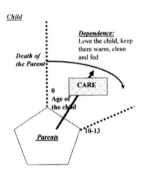

| Dot pattern - response of the Parent toward the Child. |
| Hatch Pattern - response of the Child toward Parent. |

Phase II: Ages 13-21- Honor Defined by Obedience-Illustration 2

As the child develops and begins to do things independently, the parents need to emphasize obedience and learning. The parents teach and guide the child; the child is to listen and learn. Since "foolishness is bound up in the heart of a child"[7] parents are to guide and lead with conviction and strength. The teenage years are transition years. It is the time when the child thinks he knows more than the parents, and the child has more opinions than facts. Of course this is when the child comes under the questionable influence of their peers.

The parents now must set boundaries and create in their child habits of correct behavior that will prepare and enable the child for entry into the adult world. Boundaries help the child to develop a proper world view and a truth system. These are keys to a good life. During this time, the child demonstrates honoring by obeying the parents.

The parents help the child to move from adolescence into adulthood by teaching him moral standards and to respect authority. That respect first comes from home. Don't assume a child learns respect for authority in our culture.

The relationship is still one way, thus the arrow points from the parents to the child. The parents still take the initiative to maintain the relationship. If the child does something to damage the relationship, as it was in Phase 1, it is up to the parents to restore it. By and large, a teenage child has poor interpersonal skills and needs the help and the tolerance of a loving parent to maintain the relationship.

An easy illustration of the need for parental reconciliation is the inevitability of car accident(s) when the child learns to drive. It is important not to overreact. When raising my children, I bought so many autos I thought I would eventually get a free car, had frequent purchase coupons been available!

I promise you maintaining our relationship to the children during these episodes was up to Connie and me.

Lesson 15*: When the kids are in their teen years, the parents must understand and behave like they are smarter and more experienced than the child.*

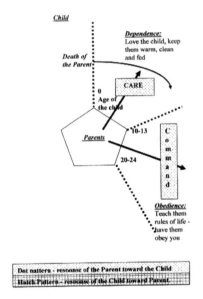

Phase III: Ages 21-35 - Honoring as Discernment- Illustration 3

Time and aging of both parties work to change the nature and dynamics in the relationship. The relationship can never be the way it was and both parties must move on to the new paradigm. The parent moves from commanding and teaching the child into counseling the child. Leadership for the daughter should be transferred from the parents to her husband and leadership for the son should be transferred from the parents to the spiritual elders in his life.

This transition is necessary for the relationship to stay well balanced. For the first time the relationship becomes two-way; thus, the arrow points from the child to the parent and from the parent to the child. Both parties must work now to keep the relationship going.

Each of our three children received counseling and suggestions in a different way. One would listen, take time to respond and then speak to the issue days later. One would hear and react immediately. And the last one would just blow it off at the first blush but would take the idea under advisement. But we persevered for the benefit of each child. We could not change how they responded, so it was important to us to adjust to them so that we could get maximum return from our suggestions.

Adult children must gain relational skills within the family and outside in society. They should be able to keep the relationship going as all parties begin to transition into this mutual participation relationship. The children must realize the parent/child relationship is good, to their best interest and required. The parents lead by counseling, suggesting and coaching. The children show honor by discernment of good and evil, by leaving and cleaving to their spouses, by demonstrating an attitude of being teachable, and by an expressed desire for the relationship. Honoring is growing up and living with discernment and the taught values. This shows the maturing process.

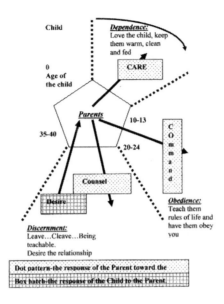

Child

Dependence:
Love the child, keep
them warm, clean
and fed

CARE

0
Age of
the child

Parents

10-13

35-40

20-24

C
o
m
m
a
n
d

Counsel

Desire

Obedience:
Teach them
rules of life and
have them obey
you

Discernment:
Leave…Cleave…Being
teachable.
Desire the relationship

Dot pattern-the response of the Parent toward the

Box hatch-the response of the Child to the Parent

Phase IV: Ages 35- 55 - Honor as Appreciation- Illustration 4

Changes become more dramatic and more difficult for the parent/child relationship during this period. As the parents approach their older years they experience reduced capacity. It is hard on the parents because they ain't what they use to be. The parents begin to fall behind in current technologies and culture. When they were younger, the parents could name all the movie stars and singers and handle all the technologies. Now, however, they know little of whom the stars are, what the music is and how the technology works. Moreover, they couldn't care less about knowing; being current and on top of society is just not interesting anymore to them. Honor by the child becomes an attitude of appreciation for the parents for who they are and who they were. The child must recognize the parents are in the process of finishing up their lives. The child needs a desire to maintain the relationship with the parents and needs to work to adjust to the parents. The relationship is starting to converge as the child becomes more of the initiator. This time the arrow points from the child to the parent. The child must cultivate the relationship for it to continue to stay viable. The parents still need to work at the relationship but the child is becoming the dominate force in the relationship and often the grandchildren become the focus. This cultivation period is mandatory for both the child and the parents. It is important for the child to develop the right perspective for the coming years; this is true of the parents also.

This period is difficult when someone comes from a dysfunctional home. The child may feel the parent does not deserve his attention or honor. If we review the command again, we will see there is no caveat or escape clause. All are to honor their parents. It is now becoming the child's responsibility regardless of the history of the relationship.

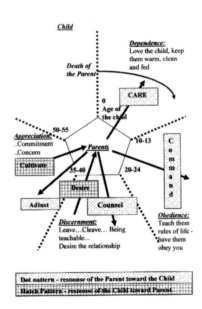

Phase V. Ages 55 for the child and on - Honor as Role-Reversal-Illustration 5

Bill Garrison, a wise friend of mine, says that as babies we had four needs: to be loved, to be kept warm, to be clean and to be fed. When we have reached old age, we again need four things: to be loved, to be kept warm, to be clean and to be fed. As we get older, we come full circle from parents caring for the children to the children caring for the parents. This role reversal is hard for all parties. None of us have the desire or training to become our parent's parent or the parent becoming the child's ward.

Also, the aged parent may not be able to maintain a relationship due to diminished capacity, and so it is the child's responsibility to be sure the relationship is maintained.

Lesson 16: All the money in the world will not substitute for personal attention and love of a child to an aging parent. It is up to both child and parent to make this transition as a function of commitment and not just of resources.

When visiting Mother at the nursing home late in her life, it was interesting to note how the people lined up for food long before it was served. Their whole lives revolved around the schedule of sleeping, eating and watching TV. This was true of Eva when she lived with us. This was the extent of her living circle. As we get older we contract our life to a tight, small circle. Diminished capacity as we get older drives us to implode our paradigm. The children become the major contact with reality left for the parent.

Also as people get older, the idiosyncrasies of their younger years become more extreme and dominant. We call it becoming eccentric. If the parents exaggerate a little when they are young, they will exaggerate a lot when they get older. Traits become extreme.

I noted that many parents as they aged became more and more foul-mouthed. When visiting the nursing home I was always taken aback by the language of the older people. All inhibitions are gone and they tend to let it fly!

Lesson 17: Age brings on eccentric behavior and a foul mouth.

The activities of honoring are an expression of your attitude of your parents' worth. It comes from your decision to treat your parents as though they have value. It is making sure the parents know they are appreciated. We are to be committed to our parents' well being and exhibit concern for their well being. It is not enough to say we are concerned; we must also exhibit concern and a life style that includes them in our lives. As we started with our parents caring for us, we end with us caring for our parents.

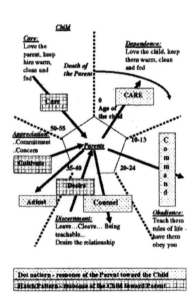

Summary

Illustration 5 is only a general representation of what we experience as we progress through life. The age spans will vary based on a number of factors, such as health, financial capacity, personal history and personality attributes; but the concept of a changing set of needs over time is valid and deserves our consideration. Both parents and children must adjust with the changing environments. We need the correct relationship for each stage in our lives.

Here are nine observations I made from the illustration:

Lesson 12: If children do not have application for honoring their parents in their youth, they will most likely not understand the command to honor in their later years.

Lesson 18: How we responded to our parents in our teens will not work when we are in our 40's. Our response must change with our aging to facilitate the relationship and to honor our parents.

Lesson 19: If you do not honor your parents, your children are watching.

Lesson 20: The relationship between a parent and child is a changing vista of emotions and responsibilities, and each must take responsibility for the relationship. This is a relationship God values and we would be wise to work at it. And it does take work.

Lesson 21: The parent/child relationship is circular. It starts with the parents caring responsibility and ends with the child caring responsibility; the responsibility has shifted from parent to child, to child for parent.

Lesson 22: There is a special emphasis from God on this relationship and we must be sure to obey by doing our part.

Lesson 23: The relationship will survive when each party plays their role to make it work.

Lesson 24: The relationship and service of the child to the parent cannot be motivated out of guilt

Lesson 25: Forgiveness does not minimize the wrong doing; forgiveness and trust in God are keys to all relationships.

Lesson 26: The honoring relationship is a reflection of God's plan for us. It just doesn't happen; forgiveness and love are required.

Post Script

I write this section to those with bad family histories. I personally never had the problem of a bad family life, but if you did, remember Jesus said: *"Love your enemies, do good to those who hate you, bless those who curse you, pray for those who mistreat you. Be merciful, just as your Father is merciful."*[8] Sometimes our enemies are the members of our own families. God calls us to love bad parents and forgive them whether they ask us to or not. We need to honor our parents, regardless of whether or not we think they deserve it. In doing so, we are choosing to imitate our heavenly Father, instead of our earthly parents.

A pastor friend once said: "In one of my first classes at seminary, a professor made the comment, 'We understand God within our understanding of our parents, because, in a sense, our parents *are* God to us'. It was obvious he knew the weight of the words he had spoken, but in his stoic manner he spoke as if he was making the most natural observation. And it *is* a natural observation: our parents initially shape what we learn to see."

To those who had abusive parents or parents who were never attentive to your needs, there was never any honoring model for you to witness. But despite this fact, you must still honor your parents wherever you are in the age cycle of honoring; honoring does not depend upon their performance. Additionally, you must begin to model honoring your parents for your children so the concept becomes normal behavior for your progeny. Remember, in God's economy, honoring your parents is in your best interest.

Some adult children may need to get counseling or join a support group, but the command stands irrespective of our condition. We are to find ways to obey the command, not justify walking around it. Since God gives us no options, we need to learn how to honor and not how to escape it.

Lesson 27: *The honoring relationship is a reflection of God's plan for us. It just doesn't happen; forgiveness and love are required.*

A popular phrase today is "to get closure." It is my opinion the key to getting closure is forgiveness. Forgiveness as opposed to confronting (letting others have a piece of your mind; letting them know you are hurt). Our society encourages us to say what we think of a situation rather than measure our words. This is unfortunate as it is better to guard our mouths and say what is helpful. Our words are to be edifying.

A friend of mine once had a spring picnic for the family. The friend's parent was getting old and slipping in capacity, but was brought along. During the picnic, his two-year-old granddaughter hit the table by accident and knocked over some of the ice tea on the table. All the people just laughed and helped clean up the mess. There was no scolding of the child, for everyone understood it was an accident and the child did not have the faculties or the understanding to correct the problem.

Later during the picnic, the aging parent's knee hit the table and repeated the ice tea incident. This time, however, all the adults became irritated and were put out with the parent. Their patience was nonexistent for the aging parent's mistake.

Why are we more understanding of the child than the aged parent, when we should be understanding of both? What is cute with a child is irritating with an aging parent. The problem is the child is cute and the aging parent is ugly.

Chapter 4

Family Observations

Ecclesiastes 3:1 *"To every thing there is a season, a time and a purpose under heaven."*

A fable

There is a Grimm's fairy tale about a family in which three generations lived together in the same house. The old grandfather's hand began to shake when he was eating at the table, and food would spill on his shirt and the tablecloth. The daughter-in-law began to be offended by his messiness and prevailed upon her husband to move his father to the kitchen where she would not have to watch him eat. A few weeks later they heard a crash from the kitchen and found the grandfather had dropped his plate on the floor and it had broken. The daughter-in-law was indignant at the mess and from then on served her father-in-law his food in a wooden bowl which could not be broken. One suppertime, the father noticed his four-year-old son playing with a piece of wood and asked him what he was doing. "I'm making a wooden bowl," he said, smiling up for approval, "to feed you and Mama out of when I get big." The father and mother looked at each other for a while and didn't say anything. Then they cried a little. Then they went into the kitchen and took the grandfather by the arm and led him back to the dining table. They sat him in a comfortable chair and gave him his dinner on a china plate, and from then on nobody scolded when he clattered his silverware, or spilled his food, or broke things.

The following observations are true when you are dealing with an aging parent. The last living parent is traumatic because there is no support from the parent's spouse and because of its finality to your history.

Forces of the last days

When my brother and I were going through Mother's transition during her last days, there were at least seven people/forces that influenced and put pressure on the decisions and courses of action we made:

1. There was Mother. Even though mentally incapacitated, my mother had needs we knew intuitively and through our history with her.
2. There was my sibling. We had different values and different spouses and different experiences between us. We had not made any joint decision since Dad's death twenty years earlier and this experience was difficult and uncomfortable at best.
3. There was my brother's wife.
4. There was my wife. Connie was the mother of three children, the wife of a husband who had started his own business and the daughter of a mother who was also slipping into old age.
5. There were my kids. They were in their teenage years and required our attention and time, time, time.
6. There was the church society with its opinions.
7. There was the estate.

I found that the first six had personalities, emotions and opinions on how Mother's needs were to be met. (This was also true of Connie's mom.) At the same time, Connie and I felt we had the responsibility to be sure that biblical honor was carried out for our mothers.

The Sibling's View

My brother and I were in our early 40's when the problem with Mother became evident. When we realized the issue, we both postured ourselves in readiness to serve her.

It was during this time that Bill Garrison told me that at birth we have four needs: to be loved, kept warm, cleaned and fed. It was also his conclusion as we exit life, we return to those same four needs: to be loved, kept warm, cleaned and fed. Even though this comment was reviewed in the previous chapter, it is worth restating. It is the full circle of life.

This was a surprising truth to me and upon reflection; I had to agree with Bill's observation. In thinking how to apply my course of action in accordance with this truth, I thought I could hire out the functions of feeding and keeping clean and keeping warm. But I could not hire out being loved. My conclusion was that only I could provide the love my mother required. The love was not so much doing for her but nurturing her.

While I was considering the love required by my mother, I had a session with Lorne Sanny of the Navigators and he told me a story of his sitting with a man who was dying. The man had only days to live and lay alone in his hospital bed. Lorne said he thought and prayed about what he could say or read to the man. With the man's leading, he concluded that what the man wanted most of all was to be touched by another human being. Lorne concluded that the road to one's death is lonely and human touch is important. I concluded this was to be my job and pleasure with Mother. This was a job I could not delegate; therefore I focused on loving her. To me, honor meant meeting her need for love.

Lesson 28: The road to one's death is lonely and human touch is important.

My brother disagreed with the concept of me being the love provider and hiring out the rest. I think he felt that love was better expressed in the detail of cleaning her, feeding her and keeping her warm. This is a legitimate position. I felt I could hire out the feeding and keeping her clean but I should preserve my strength to give her all the attention and affection and touching she needed. This concept I adopted, and it contributed to my brother and I having strife in the process of honoring mother. What honor looked like became a source of contention.

The method of execution of honoring the parent can be the source of much contention. Siblings do not always agree on how to do this, but the disagreement should not turn into a battle. We must remember to keep the focus on the parent and not on winning an argument. An agreed-to strategy is preferable to contention but not always possible. All parties of the family should contribute but not all need to contribute equally. It appears silly to me to have strife on the how-tos as long as the objective of honoring is accomplished.

I think my brother felt Connie and I were cold, unfeeling and negligent because we did not sign up for all of Mother's caring needs, including feeding, keeping clean, and keeping warm. He never said this, it is only my speculation. Parenthetically, my brother's position was the same position held by some of the other groups with whom we were friends.

Mother's View

Mother was not a demanding woman, so when she lost her ability to dictate her desires my brother and I pretty much decided all things. We got a power of attorney early on in her illness and limited her driving, doing banking, etc. As Mother worsened and experienced complete diminished mental capacity, my brother and I became her caregivers. We shared having Mother live with us over the ensuing years. For the record, my brother kept her more time than I.

Much to my chagrin, when Mother was with me, I had to bathe her, towel her after her shower, cut her toenails and comb her hair with the help of my wife. The thing I hated to do the most was cutting her toenails. There was just something about it that freaked me out.

Dealing with your parent in such vulnerable positions as bathing, toweling down and cleaning up is uncomfortable. It does require your commitment and focus to stay with the process. This kind of exposure can offend a modest parent and is a sensitive time for all parties. However, Mother was so debilitated by this time, I am not sure it registered with her.

When Mother first stayed at our house, she would get up during the night and try to wander off. Other times she would get disoriented in her bedroom and I would awaken to find her stranded in an empty bathtub. Many nights I would have to bail her out of the problems she had gotten herself into. It go so bad that I had to lock her in her room at night. I did not like having to restrict her and I was concerned with the potential fire consequence from such a move. Her room was right above our room and every noise of movement could be detected. The kids slept on the same floor as Mother and her handicap was distracting to say the least. None of us were getting any sleep. This could not go on.

In the last months of her life we decided to put Mother in a nursing home. This decision was driven by our available resources: our time, energy, money, and emotional and physical capacity. These resources were all we had to apply to the problem and to handle our other responsibilities. Mother could afford modest professional care and she got the best from me for the energy and time I had available. Mother was not aware when she went into a home, but with parents who are aware this is a very difficult time. Cognizant parents know that the only probable way out of the home is death. But there are circumstances when we, as the child, must make this necessary decision.

In effect my mother became my ministry and the outlet for my tithing. My time and energy were the determinants on what I considered reasonable care. I realized I could only *care to my capacity*. If she required more than I had, then something had to give. Since I could not fix the problem caused by her aging, this was what my application for the command Honor your Parent became.

Lesson 29: Aging parents are not like the child. The more energy put into the child, the more the child grows and develops. This is not true for the aging parent. There is no reciprocal growth in the parent for the time invested; the parent is a depreciating asset. The child must love and support without expectations. The parent will continually and gradually slip out of the child's hands to the grave.

Mother was a very important priority in our lives. But there were other people who also had a call on our lives. When Connie and I made the commitment to honor our mothers, there were other relational commitments we continued to handle. We could not handle them at the expense of our mothers and we could not handle our mothers at the expense of other commitments. For instance, I could not sacrifice my wife for my relationship to my mother, and I could not sacrifice my mother for the sake of my wife; I had to live in balance with both of them. Also, I could not decide on being mediocre in both relationships. However, there were commitments we could compromise on, such as church attendance, work schedules, civic affairs, friendships, and tithing. Likewise, we had to work with my brother in the care of my mother.

The truth was still honoring my parent. The application was for me to love her and care to my capacity. The applications sometimes created strife.

Lesson 30: Truth does not vary but application does.

When I quit smoking because of the truth, "Your body is the temple of God,"[9] I did not break off my relationship with others who smoked. But the application of honoring parents tends to create strife among siblings and may eventually break the relationship.

Lesson 31: There are little if any victories or revelations that "solve the problem" of aging because the problem cannot be solved. The aging process marches to an inevitable end and we are just caught up in the process.

During Mother's care, I reduced my schedule and responsibilities as much as I could and there was no slack left over. Connie and I concluded the boys still had to carry on with school and enjoy their sports and other activities. Our daughter still had to go to dance lessons. We could not stop life for the dying process. Though we gave up any hope of participating much beyond being a spectator in the boys' sport leagues, we still supported them with time and energy. We put off things of personal interest but the running and maintenance of our family could not be stopped or compromised.

Therefore with my schedule, I would visit Mother once or twice a day, three to five times per week. Connie would see her during the week when I was not available and pick up the slack for me. The children went with me every weekend and sometimes during the week. I met with the nursing home management a few times per week to let them know I was watching. We had friends with parents in the same home and we would switch off to say hello to the other's parent to ensure a feeling of being visited. It was our expression of care.

Connie and I concluded after much prayer and thought that honoring is *caring to your capacity* and only you can determine your capacity. My brother and I might have disagreed in the application, but I think we both agreed on the truth — honor your parent.

Lesson 32: *In the last years, honor to your parents is expressed by caring to your capacity.*

There are a lot of abandoned parents when the decision by the family is to do nothing. There is no excuse for this decision. To the other extreme, being a martyr is not virtuous. There is no formula in the Bible on how much to do or what to do. Each of us has to make the decision on how to honor our parent and will answer to God in heaven for that decision. The Bible does not call us to destroy our lives in dealing with a parent problem but we are not justified in not facing the issue.

When God asks you the question, "Did you honor your parent?" are you confident of your answer? My decision was to care for Mother to my capacity, which meant loving her. As noted earlier, I felt I was the one to give her love but decided other things could be hired out. If you cannot afford to do this, then you and your siblings must:

1. Pull together and develop a strategy of time commitment with each other
2. Study and get governmental help
3. Or use the estate to meet your parents' needs.

Remember love may be no more than holding them in your arms and comforting them, combing their hair, clipping their toenails or feeding them in the cafeteria. Only you can make the decision.

Lesson 29: Aging parents are not like the child. The more energy put into the child, the more the child grows and develops. This is not true for the aging parent. There is no reciprocal growth in the parent for the time invested; the parent is a depreciating asset. The child must love and support without expectations. The parent will continually and gradually slip out of the child's hands to the grave.

The Spouse's View

A key to this journey is mutual commitment and support among the spouses. My wife committed herself to the journey early on and stayed with me as I dealt with the difficult decisions. She believed the command to honor my mother was also her responsibility. Connie's mother moved in with us in September and my mother died the ensuing March. Therefore, there was an overlap in caring for the two mothers. With Mother's death, we started a whole new siege with Eva for another twelve years. It was important that Connie and I were mutually committed to the honoring process for both parents.

Lesson 33: The rule is my parents are for my spouse to honor and my spouse's parents are for me to honor.

Remember, honoring is very much attitudinal; the transaction is care to your capacity. It will take different forms with different families but all parents merit honoring via the command of God.

The Children's View

During one of my visits to the nursing home with the kids, I told Mother I loved her and that she had been a good mother. I then turned to my children and said that even if she did not understand me at all, I wanted both her and them to hear my feelings. At that moment Mother sat up in bed and said, "Yes, I do hear you and it matters," and then she sank back into her pillow and back into the black hole. My children and I sat stunned. Somehow she had pulled herself back from the abyss to tell me she was there just before I lost her again, this time for life. It was 1988. She died a month later at 80 years of age.

Both my wife and I felt it necessary for our children to experience the journey of the aging of both mothers. Also, we expected the kids to go on with their lives and "let the dead bury their own dead".[10] We wanted our children to have healthy memories of their grandmothers but we also wanted them to taste reality. Of course we did not expose them to all matters but included them in the inevitable process to death. For instance, the kids would take a vigil with Connie or me at the nursing home or hospital but they were never engaged in things such as incontinence. In the ensuing years it became apparent this exposure had impacted our children and helped clarify how they should handle us in similar circumstances. We felt the modeling of honor was an important responsibility.

Our children experienced the ugliness of losing one's mind, nursing home situations and at the same time the miracle of God in my mother. The story of the momentary awakening of Mother, as told earlier, was a magic moment we still review today. Our children saw in Eva the loss of physical capacity and the harvest of bad habits from youth. And yet they have a great respect for their grandparents. Both mothers' lives were great lessons for the children in the inevitability of aging and the need for good relationships with all members of the family. Both mothers modeled courage, gratitude and love.

Old age, death and elderly people are not pretty in the physical state. The golden years are not very golden. Old people smell, nursing homes stink of ammonia and the scene is less than beautiful, but it is reality. Children must see and understand this part of life also. The end of life's journey is not always beautiful and "happily ever after."

Lesson 17: *Age brings on eccentric behavior and a foul mouth.*

Modeling honoring is a key to the children's maturation process. Remember the truth never varies but application does.

Lesson 19: *If you do not honor your parents, your children are watching.*

After Mother died I always intended to go back and help the abandoned elders at the nursing home, but I never could conjure up the courage to do it. To face the odor of death was more than I could handle. I admire those who do this ministry. They are a unique lot and deserve our prayers and thanks.

Grandparents

My studies also made me conclude in the case of your parent's death or negligence of your grandparents by your parents, the grandparents could become your responsibility. Remember God puts special emphasis on the care of widows and older people.

Money and Inheritance among the Siblings

My parental grandfather died in June of 1958. He was the last of my father's parents and so the remaining estate was settled and disbursed. It was the selling off of the properties of an 80-year-old man and his work.

My mother died in 1988, some 30 years later. When she died, she was the last of the parents and the estate was settled and all things were disbursed or sold off. They were the properties of an 80-year-old woman and what was left from her life.

During the estate settlement for Mother, my paternal uncle called and said there had been an heirloom, rightfully his, which my dad had taken when their father died. My uncle wanted it back because it belonged to him. When we inquired what it was he had been missing these 30 years, he told us it was a butter dish. The thorn in his memory of my dad was a butter dish! This must have caused him distress over these 30 years for him to remember it and resurrect it at the settling of Mother's estate. (Don't laugh — you have your own butter dish.)

I do not think less of my uncle for this transaction, but it is an illustration of how an estate can be a relational killer in a lot of cases. The question we must ask ourselves is what is our butter dish? Is our relationship worth a butter dish?

After going through the trials of an aging and dying parent, I came to the conclusion money has the potential to mess up any relationship. Anything between $1 and $1,000,000,000 can create conflict among the siblings and other members of the family.

Lesson 34: Money-inheritance can be a family wrecker no matter how large or small the estate.

Money is an area of much angst. Because the settlement of the estate is the last act of honoring by the children, problems from the estate settlement should not besmirch the parents' life or memory. We should not fight amongst ourselves or be jealous and suspicious of each other.

To let you know this is not a new issue, revisit

Luke 12:13-15: *"13 Then one from the crowd said to Him, "Teacher, tell my brother to divide the inheritance with me." 14 But He said to him, "Man, who made me a judge or an arbitrator over you?" 15 And He said to them, "Take heed and beware of covetousness, for one's life does not consist in the abundance of the things he possesses."*

Sound familiar?

Even though Mother's estate was modest, it was adequate for her needs. Yet my brother and I developed hard feelings during the management of the estate settlement. I must say I think he settled it fairly by the end, but there were many times in the middle that both he and I were upset. It destroyed what was left of our relationship.

My wife and I decided the only way we could honor our mothers was to have no designs on the estate. It meant if we received nothing of the estate we would be fine. The primary objective was to honor the parent and not worry about getting our fair share. We concluded if the estate, no matter what the size, was in the forefront of our thinking, we could not honor our parents. With the estate at the forefront we would manipulate the family and circumstances rather than operating in the best interest of our parents.

As we talked with many families over the years in similar situations, the advice we gave was to hold everything with an open hand before God, without expectations of getting anything from the estate. This relinquishing of ownership or getting at least a fair share is hard to swallow and apply, but I never met anyone who did not agree with the conclusion. However, I still struggled with this truth over Mother's modest estate, before and after she died.

Lesson 35: To sustain the attitude of honoring, one must relinquish any design on or ownership of things in the estate.

When Mother died, a respected counselor friend of mine suggested I sue my brother for a settlement. However, I was convinced whatever was left of our relationship would be destroyed by this action. No estate is worth the damage a legal suit would bring.

> *"For you know the grace of our Lord Jesus Christ that though He was rich, yet for your sakes He became poor, that you through His power you might become rich."[11]*

The question in following Jesus' example is am I willing to become poor for someone's righteousness? To guard against losing this perspective, we must ask ourselves, "What is my butter dish?"

If Connie and I have our way, we will divvy up most of our possessions by some scheme before our demise. We have also been advised to have an annual family discussion to review the status of the estate to set expectations. Hopefully this will cause us to be the bad guys in the eyes of the kids and not each other.

The major idea is to not let the estate become an issue between the kids. The assumption that the kids' good relationship will offset a struggle, a rift or hard feelings is naive. Money and things can be a relationship killer.

A will is important, but having a sit down divvy up and set expectations explanation is just as important. Estates do not necessarily bring joy to the children. There is always someone who thinks he has been ignored or slighted. He is sure he did more and thus deserves more than the others. Therefore it is best to talk it out beforehand and let your children know your love and your thinking. Most parents will not do this. I have heard more than one say, "Let the kids work it out after I am gone." This is a shortcut to family division. I strongly encourage a pre-death strategy session(s). This should be done irrespective of the size of the estate. This would include the scenario of how the estate is run in case the husband departs ahead of the wife.

I have heard it said there must be an equal distribution of the estate. This sounds good in theory but is unrealistic. At the very least, the children's needs and your history will determine the proportion of the distribution.

I have gotten good advice from numerous financial counselors about strategies for estate discussion and dispersal. They have also told me first-hand stories of the problems they have witnessed in the settling of estates, and I was fear struck. The Ron Blue Associates or Merrill Lynch would be helpful in any person's planning. Notice, I do use advisors. This is not a trail to walk alone. Be sure to have good counselors.

Lesson 2: With all the complexity of retirements, estates and taxes, you will need all the experts you can get.

Money and the Aging Parent

Three things are true:

One: As parents age, they lose their ability to earn money. They are on a fixed asset and income basis. This status of fixed asset level will cause concern and angst with the parents. They have no capacity to recover from a setback and this is scary to them.

Lesson 36: The elderly widow has no capacity to make any more money. Any time you fiddle with her money it scares her.

Two: As parents age, they become suspicious and certain someone is stealing from them. A lot of time the someone suspected of stealing is their child. Don't take it personally unless you are guilty. Even my mother concluded we were stealing her money.

Lesson 37: Most elderly or widowed parents think at one time or another that their child is stealing their money

Three: The siblings become suspicious of each other's motives in the handling of the money. This is also true of the spouses-in-law. Just review the movie *Sense and Sensibility* to see it displayed for you.

Death of One Parent before the Other

Both Connie's father and my father died young so this is the environment in which I spent over 30 years of my life. In regard to my brother and me dealing with Mother, my conclusion is we would have been better off had we had an executor administering Mother's income to keep her on a monthly salary. The minute both my brother and I became involved, it was always a struggle of who knew best. The truth of it is, neither one of us was very smart in financial matters.

Don't get tricky with your parent's money. Don't let siblings get tricky with your parent's money. It is best, if at all possible, to construct the estate so the parent can use it and spend it. If parents can take care of themselves, let him be. Who cares if all the money is used in the process? It is the parent's money and not yours. People justify a lot of cruel decisions in the name of stewarding Dad/Mother's money.

A third party administrator can keep the children free of suspicion and mutual distrust. The administrator is an unbiased participant in financial decisions, without a personal agenda in administering the estate. Administrators cost money but they are worth it.

Lesson 2: With all the complexity of retirements, estates and taxes, you will need all the experts you can get.

Believer Sibling to Non-Believing Sibling

As the reader can observe from earlier in this chapter, my sibling was rarely happy with what I did or how I did it. There was an air of distrust in his view of the way I wanted to help Mother. This distrust ran both ways and hindered our relationship. My commitment to honor Mother by my love did not assure me of my brother's acceptance or respect on what I did or how I did it. We never agreed on the application of honor and this difference created a strained relationship. I must say I was as guilty as he in not operating and communicating on the differences. The shame of it all is this misunderstanding hurt our relationship. This is the last thing Mother and Dad would have wanted.

The description of the interaction above is normative for believers and non-believers alike. It is true for any combination of siblings. This period is one of stress and division.

A believer should expect little to no understanding or agreement of the biblical concept of honor from a non-believing sibling. Non-believers will tend to see the relationship to the parent from their perspective and values only. This should be expected. There is no fixed system or algorithm on how to honor a parent. There are no cultural norms to observe and study. Honoring begins with a value system and personal attitude towards the parents; actions flow from those attitudes and viewpoints.

The attitude of conferring value to the parent takes supernatural help, especially if there has been abuse or the parent is simply hard to love. The worse the family history, the more complex this issue becomes.

Lesson 38: Love in the case of honoring your parents is an act of the will and not just an emotion. Love is a good word, but the emotions of "loving" can wear out in the long journey to the grave.

The Scriptural position of honoring is a child's declaration/commitment to the value of the parent. This position is arrived at with God's help, even if the parent is no longer pretty or the care issues are no longer convenient, or if there is no money, or if it's a lifestyle interruption. But believers must remember honoring is mandatory.

All of this is to say the sibling is not the issue. All too often we believers try to convert the sibling to our way of thinking, or to the Lord, at the expense of the parent. We can still be a team with different values. We must remember the soul of our sibling is God's responsibility and the honor of our parent is our responsibility.

Lesson 39: The role of the believing child is <u>not</u> to convert his sibling out of guilt or superiority of motive, but to focus on the parents and ensure they are "honored" during these days.

Believer Sibling to Believing Sibling

Stay focused on the parent.
Don't judge each other.
Pray together for the parent.
Work together for the parent.
Hold the estate with open hands before God.
Don't be petty.

Believer to a Mother or Dad with a Dying Spouse

If at all possible, follow the parent's lead. Intercede only when necessary or the parent asks you to take over. We do not understand the emotions of losing a spouse of many years, and it is best to let the parents have his/her way.

Taking Over the Parent's Life

Lesson 40: The rule is let your parents live as long as they can on their own.

The time to take over for the parents is an invisible line where no bright line exists. My observation is most adult children try to move in on the parent too fast. They want to take over, move the parent to their town or neighborhood, and have the parent around their kids, and so on. This

romance of the moved in parent does not last long once he/
she moves close. I loved having my mother and Connie's
mother around, but they were happier with their own friends
and their own lives as long as they could manage it.

Lesson 40: <u>Continued</u> *Most children believe their parents
are much older than the parents think they are. As children,
don't move in on your parents until it is totally clear they
have lost the capacity to function.*

Once you take the living responsibilities off of the parent's
shoulders, watch out. The parent will forget how to handle or
lose the emotional capacity to handle the responsibilities of
life. Have you ever noticed that when a world-ranked athlete
steps down, he or she can never quite return to their prime? It
is called loosing the edge or desire to compete. It seems when
we decide the parent can't handle it, he or she proves us right.
Therefore, it is in the parent's best interest and yours to help,
support, and encourage an independent life. Do not remove
the parent prematurely from the responsibility of living.

I think my brother and I let Mother's independence go on
too long, but I also think I would do the same again. Mother
did not want us to take over. She was happiest fending
for herself. She did not want to give up her home and she
mentally failed a lot faster after we took over. Most aging
parents do not want to relinquish control. I know we took
Connie's mother's car away from her for good reasons when
she was 74; the driving was too difficult where we lived.
This was hard on her. She immediately became dependent
upon Connie, and Connie turned into a taxi driver for the
remaining 12 years of her mother's life.

None of these changes of control are wrong but be careful
as you progress in these decisions.

Lesson 40: <u>*Continued*</u> *Let your parents fend for themselves as long as they can—it is in the best interest of all.*

The Patriarch Syndrome

As I got into my 40's, when I was asked to tell about my family, I always started with me, and then Connie and the children. In reflection, before I was married, I always started with my grandparents or Mother and Dad. But as soon as I had my first child, the listing of my family lineage changed. The lineage started with my name and excluded Mother, Dad, and the grandparents. In other words, when I had children the family lineage became my life going forward and I had become the patriarch. It appears to me this shift in leadership cut my parents off from being critical members of the family and placed them as takers rather than givers. Even though this shift was small and subtle, it created in me a lesser view of my parents' contribution and changed the way I treated them. The lesson from the Patriarch Syndrome:

Lesson 41: Violation of honoring our parents is one of the indulgences we are entertaining in our society. Statistics indicate elder abuse is on the rise. Euthanasia is becoming a more attractive solution. But we must remember God had honoring as a cornerstone to societal stability and violation will have a devastating affect on our lives and society. Honoring our parents starts with us today, not the next generation.

Lesson 42: We should always hold our parents in high esteem to enhance our capacity to honor them.

Note the following quote: "'You shall rise before the gray headed and honor the presence of an old man, and fear your God: I am the Lord."[12]

Parents should always be considered and spoken of in the lineage. This should be done throughout our lives. The Asian culture esteems aging parents and this respect positively changes the construction of the family. From my studies this tradition of esteem seems to be waning with increased affluence in Asia.

Honoring Dead Parents

It appears to me we should honor deceased parents in our memory and conversation. We shouldn't make them out to be false heroes but we still can honor their memory. I think visiting the grave and other external signs are optional, but a mindset is not optional. Since Connie and I lost both our fathers early in our married life, our kids never knew them. The knowledge they have of their grandfathers is from our talking about them. I think it is valid to honor the deceased in our conversation.

Miscellaneous Questions and Answers

Question: Should I feel guilty if I put my parents in a nursing home?

Answer: No. The nursing home is a reality in this generation. There should be no stigma to using a nursing home; the questions that determine the correctness are when and how do I still honor them if they are out of sight?

Question: How do I make up for not doing right by my parents? *Answer:* Ask for forgiveness, train your children correctly, and help others as opportunity passes in front of you.

Question: What if there is disagreement between me and my wife on how to handle my parents?

Answer: This is the classic leadership issue. Try to work it out. Listen to her; she may be right but you must make the decision. Pray together and seek a good resolution.

Question: What if there is disagreement between me and my wife on how to handle her parents?

Answer: Where possible defer to her wishes. Pray together and seek a good resolution. Remember as her husband, you too will be responsible before God for honoring her parents.

Question: What you do in case of divorce and remarriage by the parents? How do you deal with eight parents instead of four parents?

Answer: The Bible does not comment on this complication, other than *"God hates divorce"[13]*. My studies and my intuition lead me to believe all parents are for you to honor. This is just my opinion.

Question: My parents are deceased. Is there some way I can help abandoned or neglected aging parents?

Answer: As a matter of course, one of the best ministries to widowed and abandoned parents I have ever seen is called "Adopt a Grandparent." It is a ministry in the inner city where people from other areas adopt abandoned women or men in the inner city. It is valuable and in line with the Bible. An excerpt from their Web Site is in the Appendix.

Question: How do I know when I must take over for the widowed parent?

Answer: There is no test. It is a combination of factors: the agreement of the parent if possible, sibling agreement, financial considerations, proximity, etc. Within reason, I would say the parent has 51% of the vote in this decision. The tendency is to take over too soon. Do not do that. The parent may not be as decrepit as you think.

Question: What if there is an irreconcilable disagreement between me and my sibling on how to handle the parent?

Answer: Remember there are two principles in play: one is to attribute value to the parent and second is to care to your capacity. Within reason, a great majority of all conflict can be resolved if we focus on those principles.

If the non-believing sibling is proposing that you abuse the parent, then I might go to a court of law to get it resolved.

You may find that one of the siblings does not want to help support the parent at all. If you are therefore alone remember, honor is still your command.

Chapter 5

Death

I took on the subject of death because it is the ultimate finale to honoring your parents.

The great English preacher Spurgeon once said, "Life is like a parade that passes before your eyes. It comes. Hear the people shouting. It is here. In a few minutes, people crowd the streets. Then it vanishes and is gone. Does life strike you as being just that?

"I remember, ah I remember, so many in the parade. I have stood, as it were, at a window, even though I have also been in the procession. I recall the hearty men of my boyhood, whom I used to hear pray. They are now singing up yonder.

"I remember a long parade of saints who have passed before me and have gone into glory. What a host of friends we have in the unseen world, which is 'gone over to the majority.' As we grow older, they are the majority, for our friends on earth are outnumbered by our friends in heaven.

"Some of you will fondly remember loved ones who have passed away in the parade. But please remember that you also are in the parade. Though they seem to have passed before you, you have been passing along with them, and soon you will reach the vanishing point. We are all walking in the procession. We are passing away in the land of substance and reality."[14]

Hebrews 9:27 *"And as it is appointed for men to die once, but after this the judgment."*

All the ordeals of interpersonal relationships on this earth are ended at death. *Unknown author*

Days of staying with Mom and trudging along were wearisome. And then one day it happened. I had been on a business trip and had just arrived back into town after a three day outing. It was a tiring trip to Virginia and both Chuck, my partner, and I came back exhausted. We decided to stop by the office on the way home from the airport to pick up messages and do some housekeeping. As I entered the office, a friend met me at the door and told me my mother had died at the nursing home that afternoon. I was shocked by the news and was hurt at the thought of her being gone.

Mother was no longer here and this disturbed me. I had wanted her to die and get her misery and mine over with; but at the same time, I had wanted her to never die. I was schizophrenic. On one hand, she was my mother and I was close to her. On the other hand she was not my mother anymore, being only a mere shadow of what she had been. I was conflicted over her death.

Now with both Mother and Dad dead, I was next in the parade line for the trek to death. Mother's death was the end of an era for me. My childhood past was now just my memory; there was no fleshly reality to prove it anymore. The last of my history was soon to be buried in Texas. This was both sad and a little scary. I thought on how my kids might respond to my passing.

I realize now death has little collateral damage in society; though I was sad, many other people did not care that Mom was dead. But being the person who was closely related, it is hard. The pain of death is on the ones left behind; I believe it is a blessing on the one that has gone on. A man was once asked if he was afraid of his death; he replied, "No, I am not afraid of my death. I am afraid my wife will die before me and I will be left behind."

I called my brother and told him the news. He too was sorry, but knew nothing to say at the time. We were both mute as we had both expected and desired her death, but the sadness still overwhelmed us. We were now brothers without a parent.

We spoke of burial plans and funeral arrangements. Though we'd had disagreements on Dad's funeral some 23 years earlier, we had little friction this time. Our mutual distrust had gone so far between us that now we just wanted to get this over with. We agreed to bury Mother by Dad back in our hometown of Borger, Texas. This required I ship Mother's body back home by plane.

As I saw the body the day after the death, the grief swelled back up in me again. The body that ached to be dust again was not her. She was gone. I wanted her alive again but I knew this could not be. Until I go to my eternity, I would never see my mother again. I was overwhelmed by the finality of the event of death.

On the trip back home to Texas, Connie and I flew on the same plane as Mother, but she was not in the body of the plane with us. She was in the hole with the other luggage. This caused me to have a hard, calloused and eerie feeling. Someone so vibrant and fun-loving was now just counted among the luggage. Maybe we all become luggage at some point.

The day before the funeral, as I walked through the graveyard in Borger where Mother was to be buried, I recognized the names on almost all of the tombstones. It was not only a trip down memory lane; it was sobering and sad. These were the adults of my life. They were gone and I was still here. Again I realized life marches on....to the grave.

The gravediggers had been working in preparation for the funeral and there was a hole in the ground where Mother's body was to go. There was no fantasy or anything romantic about the grave-site or the last rites. It was all functional and sterile. Within inches of where Mother's body was to be buried was my Dad's casket. It had lain there 23 years.

On the other side of Dad lay the couple who had been my surrogate parents. At the top of the graves was my grandmother's plot. Five of the most important people in my life lay in state in this ugly little graveyard in North Texas.

From this saga I began to ponder what God's view of death is. What had happened in the Garden of Eden and how does God view "the last enemy,"[15] death? If I could capture His thinking, maybe it would comfort me in my journey of transformation and grief.

First I realized my despair and grief is not what God experiences at someone's death. God has lost nothing, as all who die will come before Him. Also, if He grieved over every death, it appears to me He would change it, since He is God. There is no evidence anywhere in the Bible God grieves for the believer who dies. He may have compassion for the ones left behind but not the deceased. An example is seen in Jesus weeping for Mary at the tomb of Lazarus. He does not seem to be grieving for Lazarus but rather for the ones left behind. Jesus knew the disposition of Lazarus; He prophesized he would be awakened. God, unlike men, does not grieve over death.

My friend Walt Henrichsen noted to me that when he reviewed the Garden incident, death was one of the first gestures of grace God gave us. Here was the scene: Adam and Eve had only one command to follow. The "do not" command God gave them was not complex or tricky, but disobedience carried supreme consequences. At this time it was one strike and you are out — eat the apple and you die. Since Adam and Eve had never seen death, death could only be imagined. So, in an act of autonomy, they ate the apple anyway, and the Bible tells us this is why all mankind faces death today. We are born with the curse of death because of their sin.

After Adam and Eve's disobedience, God had a few options. He could throw Adam and Eve out and terminate all life and start over with another plan. But if God chose to start over, it would say that God was impotent and His plan had failed; defeat would not be glorifying to God.

Another option would have God saying, "I was just kidding, you have another chance." In my studying of the Bible, I see no incident where God was just kidding.

There was another option. Let Adam and Eve live with the consequence of their sinful lust for autonomy. Let them be separate from a relationship with God because of their bad behavior and let them be without a hope. God would have them die physically and spiritually.

It is evident this strategy would require another more perfect solution than the others.

All religions take a shot at this dilemma of separation from God and death, but fail because their philosophies offer no way to repair the broken relationship to God. In studying the mythical gods of Greece, you realize that their gods were capricious and unpredictable. Not so with the God of Jesus. The Bible claims that when Jesus, the Son of God, died on the cross, God solved the problem of the broken relationship. With the resurrection of Jesus from the grave, God solved the problem of death. In his death Jesus took the blame for the errors of man and therefore we are acquitted of our failings and restored to God. In other words, God took the blame for our sins. We can now relate to God. This is a divine solution. Until we experience a renewed relationship to God, we cannot answer the two great questions of man: Why am I here, and what happens when I die? The reason we cannot answer the questions without God is God is the only one with the answer.

When I was a boy, I had a paper route. Every Friday and Saturday I went door to door to collect for the last week's paper. The paper was $.25/week. The grand total of my weekly collection was $20, of which I earned $7 and gave the newspaper $13. At the end of my collections, I would go to the newspaper office to pay for the papers from the last week. One particular Saturday morning, while I was collecting for the paper, I stopped to play the pinball machine and wasted a lot of my money. When I got to the office I did not have enough money to pay the weekly bill. I told them I would pay them next week. But before I got home, someone had called my dad and reported my debt. So as you can guess, Dad had some questions when I arrived home. When confronted, I looked him in the eyes and lied, telling him that the paper company was wrong and I had paid the entire bill. Much to my surprise, Dad put me in the car and we drove to the office. Horrified, I watched as my dad took my side and declared I would not have lied to him. Dad was crest-fallen as the paper proved I had not paid. With my lie, I had broken the relationship with my dad. My behavior had driven a wedge between him and me. How was I to restore this relationship? I could not; Dad had to. He restored our relationship by paying my debt to the newspaper, telling me not to lie again, disciplining me and hugging me. I think this is what God does for me with Jesus.

God's view of death is different from ours. A review of the Psalms notes, *"Precious in the sight of the Lord is the death of His Saints.[16]"* In this verse it appears God is happy when the believer's death has occurred. How could that be? I am not happy at the death of a loved one. I think it is because

God sees the beginning from the end and knows we are with Him, not evaporated into space. Therefore, we are better off when we die than when we started out.

Revelation 2:13 *"Then I heard a voice from heaven saying to me. 'Write: Blessed are the dead who die in the Lord from now on.'" "Yes," says the spirit, "that they may rest from their labors and their works follow them."*

Death of the believer ultimately pleases God because it is the beginning of the believer's eternity and a termination of his labors in this troubled world.

Paul said, *"To live is Christ and to die is gain."*[17] The attitude that death is in our best interest appears to be a theme in the Bible. We must embrace and look to our death as a gateway to our future existence. As the Psalmist says, *"Teach me to number my days that I may gain a heart of wisdom."*[18] Face it — we always do our best work if we know there is a deadline. And there is literally a "dead" line in our life. With this eventuality, how should we to choose live?

This concept of death and its solution is counter-intuitive to our way of thinking. However, I do believe it all comes down to our perspective on this life. As I heard Howard Hendricks once ask, "Am I in the land of the living on the way to the land of the dead, or am I in the land of the dead on the way to the land of the living?" How you answer this question will determine your perspective on life and your performance in the here and now.

Ezekiel writes, *"Say to them: 'As I live says the Lord God, I have no pleasure in the death of the wicked, but that the wicked turn from his way and live. Turn from your evil ways!..?"*[19] God may be pleased with the death of His Saints, but God has no pleasure in the death of "the wicked" – those not reconciled to Him.

God has designed death so no one escapes it and there are no second chances. When we die we are dead and that is that. Our eternal destiny is between us and God. There is a consequence for what we believe and the way we have lived our life. All will face the living God and explain his or her decisions.

The Bible says there will be a judgment for nonbelievers with no hope for them. They will all go to eternal Hell without any other recourse. There will also be judgment for believers; however the difference is a judgment with hope.

1Corinthians 3:11-15: *11 "For no other foundation can anyone lay than that which is laid, which is Jesus Christ. 12 Now if anyone builds on this foundation with gold, silver, precious stones, wood, hay, straw, 13 each one's work will become clear; for the Day will declare it, because it will be revealed by fire; and the fire will test each one's work, of what sort it is. 14 If anyone's work which he has built on it endures, he will receive a reward. 15 If anyone's work is burned, he will suffer loss; but he himself will be saved, yet so as through fire."*

Believers can gain rewards in heaven or they can suffer loss in heaven. Believers will not suffer the loss of their salvation, but they can suffer loss of reward. As a believer, it does matter how I live my life after I have met Jesus. It appears there is consequence. Even though the world teaches us we can get away with it, it appears that is not so in the court of God.

The Bible teaches the totality of your life is controlled in the providence of God. Your future is not statistically governed. How many times have you witnessed the hard worker fail and the slothful worker fall into wealth? There is no cause and effect in our prosperity. If you think otherwise, ask a down-and-outer in the inner city his view of your philosophy of cause and effect. Your present status and condition is providence: your race, your nationality, your parents, your mental and physical capacity, your sex, your height, your health, the color of your eyes, etc. are all determined by God.

I remember a story we use to laugh about when I worked for IBM. The story goes that to be at headquarters (White Plains or Armonk, NY), is like being one of hundreds of ants on a log floating down a river. You could see each ant with one leg in the water kicking. If you could get your ear real close, you would hear each ant say, "I am guiding this log, I am guiding." The truth is evident.

I may be saved by grace, and I may not control my fate, but I shape the nature of my eternity by my decisions now. This gives all people across all cultures, in all circumstances, in all economic strata, hope.

Without the control of God we are at the mercy of the fickle finger of fate. That leaves us with the resolution that all of life is a roll of the dice. If we do not embrace the concepts of God's control and motivation, we must become existentialistic. This existentialistic mindset has a great tug on us in our post modernity culture. In today's culture there appears no way one could justify himself serving and honoring an aging parent. The existentialist would say, "It is my life and I will not burn it up on an old person."

It is interesting to me how society thinks it can get away with uncontrolled appetites and indulgences. We live like there are no ramifications in our life for our choices and behavior. This is true nationally and individually. However, this is antithetical to the Scriptures and is not true in any area of creation. The nihilistic attitude of me first and to hell with the rest will come home to roost. It appears to me from history that grave errors in the thinking of a culture, such as the refutation of the ways of God, play havoc with the third and fourth generation. If so, we are sabotaging our grandchildren.

I found solace in the thought God was glad to have Mother in heaven with Him. She was better off after death than living tormented life here on earth. This was not an inane platitude; I was glad for her. Though I missed her and I hurt, I could celebrate. Now all my past family is in heaven waiting for me.

Philippians 1:20-21*: "I eagerly expect and hope that I will in no way be ashamed, but will have sufficient courage so that now as always Christ will be exalted in my body, whether by life or by death. For to me, to live is Christ and to die is gain."*

Paul in Philippians sums up his motivation in the verse above. In thinking on *"To live is Christ and to die is gain,"*[20] I wonder if the song sung by Peggy Lee was not right, "Is this all there is to life"? Biblically speaking, the answer is yes.

I have three choices with my life. Choice one is to reject Jesus. Choice two is to believe Christ but live my life to optimize fun and fulfillment here on earth, and then to pass on into heaven with a modestly good conscience. Choice three is to believe Christ and get my joy in life by focusing on the things of God and serving others and reap the rewards that are promised in heaven. The third choice is a spiritual deferred annuity. My mother's death brought this into focus. After her death, she knew the truth as she faced her Creator. There was no question in her mind now. She saw Christ. She would be rewarded for time here on earth.

Was dying to her gain? If she could speak to me now, what would she say? When you face death will you be surprised by the reality of God and His judgment?

The focus and motivation has to be, *"to live is Christ.... to die is (my) gain."* Whatever years we have left should be spent living in the joy of our salvation and investing in eternal matters. We want to be sure dying is gain.

Lesson 43: *We have little to nothing to do with our salvation but we have everything to do with how we spend our life in eternity.* — *Walt Henrichsen*

Two Stories on Death

First story: Life of Job, Chapter 1

*1 There was a man in the land of Uz, whose name was Job; and that man was blameless and upright, and one who feared God and shunned evil. 2 And <u>**seven sons and three daughters**</u> were born to him. 3 Also, his possessions were <u>**seven thousand sheep, three thousand camels, five hundred yoke of oxen, five hundred female donkeys**</u>, and a very large household, so that this man was the greatest of all the people of the East.*

4 And his sons would go and feast in their houses, each on his appointed day, and would send and invite their three sisters to eat and drink with them. 5 So it was, when the days of feasting had run their course that Job would send and sanctify them, and he would rise in the morning and offer burnt offerings according to the number of them all. For Job said, "It may be that my sons have sinned and cursed God in their hearts." Thus Job did regularly.

6 Now there was a day when the sons of God came to present themselves before the Lord, and Satan also came among them. 7 And the Lord said to Satan, "From where do you come?" So Satan answered the Lord and said, "From going to and fro on the earth, and from walking back and forth on it." 8 Then the Lord said to Satan, "Have you considered my servant Job, that there is none like him on the earth, a blameless and upright man, one who fears God and shuns evil?" 9 So Satan answered the Lord and said, "Does Job fear God for nothing? 10 Have You not made a hedge around him, around his household, and around all that he has on every side? You have blessed the work of his hands, and his possessions have increased in the land. 11 But now, stretch out Your hand and touch all that he has, and he will surely curse You to Your face!" 12 And the Lord said to Satan, "Behold, all that he has is in your power; only do not lay a hand on his person." So Satan went out from the presence of the Lord.

13 Now there was a day when his sons and daughters were eating and drinking wine in their oldest brother's house; 14 and a messenger came to Job and said, "The oxen were plowing and the donkeys feeding beside them, 15 when the Sabeans raided them and took them away—indeed they have killed the servants with the edge of the sword; and I alone have escaped to tell you!" 16 While he was still speaking, another also came and said, "The fire of God fell from heaven and burned up the sheep and the servants, and consumed them; and I alone have escaped to tell you!" 17 While he was still speaking, another also came and said, "The Chaldeans formed three bands, raided the camels and took them away, yes, and killed the servants with the edge of the sword;

and I alone have escaped to tell you!" 18 While he was still speaking, another also came and said, "Your sons and daughters were eating and drinking wine in their oldest brother's house, 19 and suddenly a great wind came from across the wilderness and struck the four corners of the house, and it fell on the young people, and they are dead; and I alone have escaped to tell you!"

Let's note that when God allowed Satan to take from Job, Job lost everything:

seven sons and three daughters
seven thousand sheep,
three thousand camels,
five hundred yoke of oxen,
five hundred female donkeys.

This is a total disaster. All was gone.
At the end of the story, God restores Job to his position. God said he gave Job a double portion in return for the events of his life.

Job 42:10 *"And the Lord restored Job's losses when he prayed for his friends. Indeed the Lord gave Job twice as much as he had before."*

Let us look at the double portion God gives Job.

Job 42: 10 *And the Lord restored Job's losses when he prayed for his friends. Indeed the Lord gave Job twice as much as he had before. 11 Then all his brothers, all his sisters, and all those who had been his acquaintances before, came to him and ate food with him in his house; and they consoled* *him and comforted him for all the adversity the Lord had brought upon him. Each one gave him a piece of silver and each a ring of gold. 12 Now the Lord blessed the latter days of Job more than his beginning; for he had fourteen thousand sheep, six thousand camels, one thousand yoke of oxen, and one thousand female donkeys. 13 He also had seven sons and three daughters. 14 And he called the name of the first Jemimah, the name of the second Keziah, and the name of the third Keren-Happuch. 15 In all the land were found no women so beautiful as the daughters of Job; and their father gave them an inheritance among their brothers. 16 After this Job lived one hundred and forty years, and saw his children and grandchildren for four generations. 17 So Job died, old and full of days.*

Seven thousand sheep to **fourteen thousand sheep; three thousand camels** to **six thousand camels; five hundred yoke of oxen** to **one thousand yoke of oxen; five hundred female donkeys** to **one thousand female donkeys; seven sons and three daughters** to **seven sons and three daughters.**

Let us observe that all transactions on the animals were doubled, but the children were a simple replacement. Why was that? Did God decide to not give him double? Did He have mercy on the mother giving birth, or was it that the children were gone from earth but were still living with God? It appears to me God did give double portion with a simple replacement. There was no need to double the children on earth since the original group was in heaven and had not gone away. Someday in the future Job would be reunited with them again. People live forever, first here on earth and then in eternity.

Second story

A famous, now deceased, pastor from Philadelphia used to tell the story of the death of his wife. She died after a long and difficult battle with cancer. Both he and his children had had a rough set of months culminating with the loss of his wife/their mother.

As the family traveled to the funeral home for the viewing, they drove up to an intersection and were facing straight into the western setting sun. Of course they all were blinded and put their hands up to shield their eyes. As they waited for the light to change, a very large 18-wheeler truck passed in front of them and momentarily cast a shadow, blocking the sun out of their eyes. The pastor turned to his children and said, "Children, would you rather be hit by the truck or by the shadow of the truck?" In disbelief they answered, "Oh Dad, you know we would rather be hit by the shadow of the truck and not the truck." The pastor said, "Of course you are right and that is what Jesus did for Mother. She was hit by the shadow of death and Christ was hit by the truck."

The finishing thought is...Thank you, Jesus.

Appendix

The following is the appendix that I picked out for this book. I wanted to add in some other thoughts and poems for the reader. This is a lengthy Appendix but it takes space to get some of this in the book. The table of contents for the Appendix is:

Appendix:

Poem: This is a poem that meant a lot to me. I think it is a good capture of the feelings of an aging person and their drift in to irrelevance.

Lessons learned: I have redocumented the lessons from the book in one location. This is for the reader's convenience. You may want to add to the list your own observations or truths you have discovered.

Excerpts from a book on aging:

Adopt a Grandmother Website excerpts:. This is the ministry that was referenced in the main body of the book. The Web site tells you more about what they do and what they are committed to. This is an exceptionally effective and good group and they deserve your attention.

Jewish discussion of honoring your parents-Mitzvah Comments: This is a collection of writing from the Jewish faith. It is interesting to understand their perspective on this key issue in that they have dealt with it from a faith position for over 5000 years.

Elder Abuse: I have included excerpts from a government manual for the public. It is interesting the view of parent abuse and instructions on how to handle it.

Bible verses on death: Since death is always a big subject I have included some further reading on death as viewed in the bible..

Talk show transcript on Abusive Parents: This is a transcript from a show that spoke on the long term effect on children from the abusive parent.

Three Case Studies: I ask 3 men to write there reflections on their aging parents to share with the reader. I could have included many, many more but these will do. They do reflect the struggle they had with the parents, the children, and the siblings. They are stories from

1. From a man with a large family and a dysfunctional history
2. From a man whose father had abandon him early on only to reenter his life later on.
3. From a man who committed adultery and divorced his wife and begged his children not to abandon him.

Excerpt from a poem

"Dark days are upon me, my husband is dead.
I look at the future, I shudder with dread.
For my young are all rearing young of their own,
And I think of the years and the love that I've known.
I'm an old woman now and nature is cruel.
'Tis her jest to make old age look like a fool.
The body it crumbles, grace and vigor depart,

There is a stone where I once had a heart.
But inside this old carcass a young girl still dwells,
Ad now again my bittered heart swells.
I remember the joys, I remember the pain,
And I'm loving and living life over again.
I think of the years, all too few, gone too fast,
And accept the stark fact that nothing can last.
So open your eyes, those around me, open and see
Not a crabbed old woman...look close...see me."
Author unknown

Author: Our Mothers could have written this.

Lessons

Lesson 1: As the parent, a good attitude and gratitude about the state of affairs is mandatory for good relations with the caregiver. The parent's gratitude may be a reflection of how much you are grateful for them.

Lesson 2: With all the complexity of retirements, estates and taxes, you will need all the experts you can get.

Lesson 3: We always do things we perceive are worthwhile and in our best interest. Altruism is by in large a myth.

Lesson 4: To stay obedient to the commands, we must believe there is temporal and eternal value for us in obedience.

Lesson 5: Remember, no one in heaven will say they are glad they did not do what God commanded. No one will ultimately say they are glad they did not honor their parents.

Lesson 6: The promise associated with honoring your parent is not that you would feel good during the experience, but rather it would go well with you all your days.

Lesson 7: Your parents' value is not determined by their performance in your relationship. Their value is determined by your ascribing value to them.

Lesson 8: History shows us that money can be the bane of relationships.

Lesson 9: Not only do we need to honor our parents but also teach our children to honor us.

Lesson 10: *In each phase of our life, our relationships to our parents change and the honoring manifestation changes with it.*

Lesson 11: *The truth of a command stands the test of all circumstances and cultures.*

Lesson 12: *If children do not have application for honoring their parents in their youth, they will most likely not understand the command to honor in their later years.*

Lesson 13: *Honoring is an action driven by an attitude and shaped by circumstance.*

Lesson 14: *The good news is you get to determine what your "honoring" looks like, and the bad news is you must explain your conclusions to God.*

Lesson 15: *When the kids are in their teen years, the parents must understand and behave like they are smarter and more experienced than the child.*

Lesson 16: *All the money in the world will not substitute for personal attention and love of a child to an aging parent. It is up to both child and parent to make this transition as a function of commitment and not just of resources.*

Lesson 17: *Age brings on eccentric behavior and a foul mouth.*

Lesson 18: *How we responded to our parents in our teens will not work when we are in our 40's. Our response must change with our aging to facilitate the relationship and to honor our parents.*

Lesson 19: *If you do not honor your parents, your children are watching.*

Lesson 20: *The relationship between a parent and child is a changing vista of emotions and responsibilities, and each must take responsibility for the relationship. This is a relationship God values and we would be wise to work at it. And it does take work.*

Lesson 21: *The parent/child relationship is circular. It starts with the parents caring responsibility and ends with the child caring responsibility; the responsibility has shifted from parent to child, to child for parent.*

Lesson 22: *There is a special emphasis from God on this relationship and we must be sure to obey by doing our part.*

Lesson 23: *The relationship will survive when each party plays their role to make it work.*

Lesson 24: *The relationship and service of the child to the parent cannot be motivated out of guilt*

Lesson 25: *Forgiveness does not minimize the wrong doing; forgiveness and trust in God are keys to all relationships.*

Lesson 26: *The honoring relationship is a reflection of God's plan for us. It just doesn't happen; forgiveness and love are required.*

Lesson 27: *The honoring relationship is a reflection of God's plan for us. It just doesn't happen; forgiveness and love are required.*

Lesson 28: The road to one's death is lonely and human touch is important.

Lesson 29: Aging parents are not like the child. The more energy put into the child, the more the child grows and develops. This is not true for the aging parent. There is no reciprocal growth in the parent for the time invested; the parent is a depreciating asset. The child must love and support without expectations. The parent will continually and gradually slip out of the child's hands to the grave.

Lesson 30: Truth does not vary but application does.

Lesson 31: There are little if any victories or revelations that "solve the problem" of aging because the problem cannot be solved. The aging process marches to an inevitable end and we are just caught up in the process.

Lesson 32: In the last years, honor to your parents is expressed by caring to your capacity.

Lesson 33: The rule is my parents are for my spouse to honor and my spouse's parents are for me to honor.

Lesson 34: Money-inheritance can be a family wrecker no matter how large or small the estate.

Lesson 35: To sustain the attitude of honoring, one must relinquish any design on or ownership of things in the estate.

Lesson 36: The elderly widow has no capacity to make any more money. Any time you fiddle with her money it scares her.

Lesson 37: *Most elderly or widowed parents think at one time or another that their child is stealing their money.*

Lesson 38: *Love in the case of honoring your parents is an act of the will and not just an emotion. Love is a good word, but the emotions of "loving" can wear out in the long journey to the grave.*

Lesson 39: *The role of the believing child is not to convert his sibling out of guilt or superiority of motive, but to focus on the parents and ensure they are "honored" during these days.*

Lesson 40: *The rule is let your parents live as long as they can on their own.*

Lesson 40: *Continued Most children believe their parents are much older than the parents think they are. As children, don't move in on your parents until it is totally clear they have lost the capacity to function.*

Lesson 40: *Continued Let your parents fend for themselves as long as they can—it is in the best interest of all.*

Lesson 41: *Violation of honoring our parents is one of the indulgences we are entertaining in our society. Statistics indicate elder abuse is on the rise. Euthanasia is becoming a more attractive solution. But we must remember God had honoring as a cornerstone to societal stability and violation will have a devastating affect on our lives and society. Honoring our parents starts with "us" today, not the next generation.*

Lesson 42: *We should always hold our parents in high esteem to enhance our capacity to honor them.*

Lesson 43: *We have little to nothing to do with our salvation but we have everything to do with how we spend our life in eternity.* —*Walt Henrichsen*

The New York Times

For the Very Old, a Dose of 'Slow Medicine'

By ABIGAIL ZUGER, M.D.
Published: February 26, 2008

It was two decades ago that a group of culinary mavericks took a giant step backward down the evolutionary trail with the "slow food" movement. Instead of fast food produced by the assembly lines of giant consortiums, they championed products of small-scale agriculture — time-consuming to prepare, beautiful to behold, very good for you.

My Mother, Your Mother
Embracing "Slow Medicine," the Compassionate Approach to Caring for Your Aging Loved Ones. By Dennis McCullough, M.D. HarperCollins. 263 pages.

Related

Excerpts From the Book

Now (and, some might add, at last) doctors are following suit, rejecting the assembly line of modern medical care for older, gentler options. The substituted menu is not for all patients — at least not yet. For the very elderly, however, most agree the usual tough love of modern medicine in all its hospital-based, medication-obsessed, high-tech impersonality may hurt more than it helps.

In its place, doctors like Dennis McCullough, a family physician and geriatrician at Dartmouth Medical School, suggest "slow medicine" — as he puts it, "a family-centered, less expensive way."

This medicine is specifically not intended to save lives or to restore youthful vigor, but to ease the inevitable irreversible decline of the very old.

Dr. McCullough directs his book to the children of elderly parents, and he pegs it to the story of his mother. She evolved from a vital, healthy 85-year-old retiree to a feeble 92-year-old dying in <u>hospice care</u>, not from any particular disease so much as the aggressive frailty common among the oldest of old people.

His bottom line is this: It is up to friends and relatives to rescue the elderly from standard medical care. And slow medicine, like slow food, involves a lot of hard work. Readers who sign on will acquire a staggering list of tasks to perform, some of which may be just as tiring and tear-producing as chopping onions.

First, while the aging parent is still vital and lively, children must not fool themselves that this happy situation will last forever. This is the time, Dr. McCullough suggests, to reinsert themselves back into the parent's life, to show up at doctor visits and to raise unpleasant topics like advance directives and health proxies.

After few more years, it is time to address the "Should you still drive?" and "Can you still manage at home?" issues, and to help create routines that compensate for a slipping <u>memory</u> and slightly wobbly balance.

Medical crises will inevitably arise; the child must be vigilant for a hospital's bad habits when caring for elderly patients. An "advocacy team" of friends and relatives should be mustered to help protect the hospitalized parent; a wider "circle of concern" should be tapped for moral support.

Still down the road is the complex world of rehabilitation, either home-based or institutional, and the even more complex spectrum of available nursing options for the slightly impaired, the seriously impaired and those near death.

All the while, medical care for the parent should favor the tried and true over the high tech. For instance, Dr. McCullough points out that instead of a yearly <u>mammogram</u>, a manual <u>breast exam</u> may suffice for the very old, and home tests for blood in the stool may replace the draining routine of a <u>colonoscopy</u>.

The parent's doctors should be nudged to justify flashy but exhausting diagnostic tests, and to constantly re-evaluate medication regimens. The high-blood-pressure pills that are life-saving at 75 may cause problems at 95, and paid companionship or a roster of visitors may prove to be <u>antidepressants</u> at least as effective as any drug.

The pace of care should be slowed to a crawl. For doctors, that means starting medications at low doses and increasing them gradually. For children, that means learning not to panic and yell for an ambulance on every bad day. And for a good overall picture of a parent's condition, a child is well advised to ignore the usual medical and nursing jargon and to focus instead on the sound of the parent's own voice. "No one," Dr. McCullough says, "can be a bigger expert on a parent's voice than a former teenager trained in the same household."

Some standard self-help fuzziness creeps around the edges of this book, with reflections on the value of scrapbooks to preserve family memories and admonitions that "it is always the right time to say 'thank you' and 'I love you.'" Dr. McCullough's decision to call each stage of old age a "station" (as in "The Station of Crisis," "The Station of Decline" and "The Station of Prelude to Dying") may be a little too religious for some and far too reminiscent for others of the food stations at large catered events.

Instead, he might have steeled the book's spine with a few hard-headed tips for those who would valiantly try to slow the twin Mack trucks of the modern doctor and the modern hospital. How should relatives go about applying the brakes to their fast doctors without alienating them or earning for themselves the label of troublemaker? Dr. McCullough, by his own report, works in something of a paradise when it comes to geriatric care, but in many medical venues the phrase "slow down" is an obscenity.

Still, he has written a valuable book, chilling and comforting in equal measure. A similar book directed at fast doctors, fast hospital administrators and fast insurers might be the next welcome stride backward down the path.

The following are excerpts from their Web Site of Adopt a Grandmother..

Adopt-A-Grandparent Program brings into relationship seniors who need and desire a supportive relationship with caring volunteers. Seniors who live in neglected urban neighborhoods often feel a sense of isolation. A personal relationship with a younger person brings new vitality to the spirit of elders and richness to the lives of volunteers.

Mission Statement

The Adopt-A-Grandparent Program seeks to enhance the lives of seniors through Companionship, Health and Wellness, Community Involvement and Spiritual Growth and Healing producing empowered, healthy, laughter-prone individuals.

Programs

The Adopt-A-Grandparent Program is the ideal forum to exercise your gifts of loving, listening and caring for others. If you have a love for the older generation, here is an opportunity to use your creativity in service, even if you have no prior experience. The main requirement of your volunteer position with Adopt-A-Grandparent is to learn how to receive the gifts the seniors give you. This is an art that takes some doing since most of us are much better givers than receivers. There are three options for volunteer opportunities with Adopt-A-Grandparent. They are: a Friend, an On-Call Driver or a Board Member.

Honor your Father and your Mother - Jewish[21]

The great importance and significance of the *Mitzvah to honor parents is seen in the fact it is part of the Ten Commandments:

Honor your father and your mother
(Exodus 20:12, Deuteronomy 5:16)

Fear your mother and your father
(Leviticus 19:3)

In the matter of honor due to parents, the father is mentioned first; in the matter of reverence due them, the mother is mentioned first. From this we infer that both are to be equally honored and revered. Thus, whatever is said of one parent applies equally to the other parent (Kerrithoth 6:9 - 28a).

**Maimonides enumerates in addition to these commandments also three prohibitions:
  a) **not to curse one's father or mother**
  b) **no to smite one's father or mother**
  c) **that a son shall not rebel against the authority of his father or mother**
(Sefer Hamitzvot II:218, 219 and 195, and Hilchos Mamrim ch 5ff.)

The Mitzvah of Kibud Av va-Em (the precept to honor father and mother) may be a self-evidently rational, ethical principle. But the Talmud refers to it as the most difficult Mitzvah[22].

Respect for parents - A religious principle

However, the fact that the Torah declares the proper child-to-parent relationship to be a Divine precept lends it a new character.

"Honor your father and your mother as the L-rd your G-d has commanded you."

(Deuteronomy 5:16)

The fact that "to honor" and "to revere" parents are Mitzvot of the Torah impresses upon these precepts a stamp of absoluteness and makes of them independent principles. Indeed, the Torah's absolute precepts remain in force even in relation to parents who may have forsaken the Torah (Hilchot Mamrim 5:12ff., and 6:11; Shulchan Aruch, 240:18).

The religious aspect of honoring parents

The commandment to "honor your father and your mother" is part of the first of the two tablets in the Ten Commandments. This is rather significant. For the precepts on the first tablet deal with typically religious matters of the man-G-d relationship, while the Mitzvot on the seConnied tablet deal with the matters related to intra-human relationships. The child-parent relationship is analogous to, and intricately bound up in, the man—G-d relationship. This is so because in bringing a child into this world the parents are in a partnership with G-d: the material substance is derived from the parents, while G-d grants spirit and soul, the vital form of man (Kidushin 30b, Nidah 31a). That is why this commandment appears in the middle of the Ten Commandments: it mediates between the first four and the latter five precepts because it is related to both groups. It is as much a religious principle as it is a social one.

When not to obey - An exception

The fact that the precepts to honor and revere parents are commands of G-d implies not only the wide extent and significance of these Mitzvot, but also their limitation. It is G-d who prescribes these Mitzvot, and it is G-d's Torah which delineates their specific details.

"'Ye shall fear every man his mother and his father, and ye shall keep my Sabbaths; I am the L-rd your G-d." Scripture juxtaposes the observance of the Sabbath to the fear of one's father in order to teach you that "although I admonish you regarding the fear of your father, yet if he bids you to desecrate the Sabbath do not listen to him [and the same is the case with any of the other commandments], for 'I am the L-rd your G-d' - both you and your father are equally bound in duty to honor Me. Do not, therefore, obey him if it results in disobeying My words.'" (Rashi on Leviticus 19:3, Yevamot 5b, Bava Metzia 32a). If parents would order their child to transgress a positive or a negative command set forth in the Torah, or even a command which is of rabbinic origin, the child must disregard the order. This includes the duty of studying Torah which supersedes that of honoring parents (Hilchot Mamrim 6:12f., Shulchan Aruch, 240:12f and 25).

Children's Behavior and Parents' Honor

Everyone must keep in mind that his personal behavior reflects very much on his parents.

Where one leads an exemplary life, this is a source of joy and honor to his parents and causes others to praise them and admire them. Conversely, a child's improper behavior is a source of disgrace and anonymity to parents, in their own eyes and in the eyes of others. (Berachot 17a, Yoma 86a, Ketubot 45a).

And just as the child has responsibilities towards its parents, the parents have definite duties and responsibilities towards their children. Foremost among the parent's duties toward his offspring is to teach him Torah, to guide him and to prepare him for a committed and meaningful Torah-life. (Talmud, Kidushin 29a).

But though the failures of the parents in their duties is often casually related to the failures of the child, by no means does this exempt or excuse the child's neglect of his own responsibilities. The Torah decrees that where the parent neglects to teach his child, the child must teach himself and on his own seek to acquire the knowledge essential to a life in accordance with the Torah. (Shulchan Aruch, Yoreh Deah, 245:1).

In addition to the various laws cited in the previous paragraphs,

1. One must be extremely careful to honor and revere his father and mother, for the
2. Torah compares it to the honor and reverence of G-d.
3. Both man and woman are enjoined to honor and revere parents. However, a married woman is not in a position to supply her parents with their needs inasmuch as she depends on others, and she is therefore exempt thereof. But she is obligated to do for her parents all she can as long as her husband does not object.
4. One must honor and respect his step-mother during his father's lifetime and his step-father during his mother's lifetime. It is proper that one honor and respect them even after the death of one's own parents.
5. One must honor and respect his father-in-law and his mother-in-law (as we find that King David honored King Saul, who was his father- in-law, by calling him "my father"; see I Samuel 24:12). Likewise one must honor and respect grandparents. Also implied in this

Mitzvah is that one must honor his elder brother and sister.

6. If the father or mother is asleep and the key to one's store lies under their pillow, one must not waken them even if he should loose much profit thereby. However, if the father would benefit by being awakened, and if the son should fail to awake him he will grieve over the loss of the profit, it is the son's duty to arouse him since that will make the father happy. It is also the duty of children to arouse their father for the performance of any religious duty (which might otherwise be neglected) as all are equally bound to honor the Almighty.

7. If the mind of his father or mother is affected, one should make every effort to indulge the vagaries of the stricken parent, until G-d will have mercy on the affected. But if the condition of the parent has grown worse and the son is no longer able to endure the strain, he may leave his father or mother provided he delegates others to give the parent proper care.

8. When a child sees his parent violate the Torah he must not say to him "You have violated a command of the Torah"; he should rather say: "Father, is it not written in the Torah thus and thus?", speaking to him as though he were consulting him instead of admonishing him, so that the parent may correct himself without being put to shame.

9. The Torah is rigorous not only with respect to him who strikes or curses his parents but also with him who puts them to shame. For he who treats them with contempt, even by using harsh words against them, even by a discourteous gesture, is cursed by G-d, as it is said: "Cursed be he that dishonors his father or his mother." (Deuteronomy 27:16)

10. One must honor his parents even after their death. When mentioning parents after their demise one should add: "May his (or her) memory be a blessing."

11. Although children are commanded to go to the aforementioned lengths in their relationship to their parents, the parent is forbidden to impose too heavy a yoke upon them, to be too exacting with them in matters pertaining to his honor, lest he cause them to stumble. He should forgive them and shut his eyes, for a parent has the right to forego the honor due him.

From the *Ahavat Israel* web site, dated April 2006:

Mitzvah (Hebrew: מצווה, "commandment"; plural, *mitzvot*; from צוה, *tzavah*,

"Command" is a word used in Judaism to refer to (a) the commandments, of which there are believed to be 613, given in the Torah (the first five books of the Hebrew Bible) or
   (b) Any Jewish law at all.
The Rabbis came to assume that the Law comprised 613 commandments. According to Rabbi Simlai, as quoted in the Talmud, this enumeration of 613 commandments was representative of

365 negative commandments like the number of days in the solar year, and 248 positive commandments like the number of bones in the human body - Talmud, tractate Makkoth 23b

For a time, gematria was a significant feature in religious thought, and so it became said that 611, the gematria value for *torah*, was the number of commandments given via

Moses, with the remaining two being identified as the first commandments of the Ethical Decalogue, given by the mouth of God Himself.

According to R. Ismael only the principal commandments of these 613 were given on Mount Sinai, the remainder having been given in the Tent of Meeting. According to R. Akiba they were all given on Mount Sinai, repeated in the Tent of Meeting, and declared a third time by Moses before his death. According to the Midrash, all divine commandments were given on Mount Sinai, and no prophet could add any new one (Midrash Sifra to Leviticus 27:34; Talmud, Yoma 80a).

In rabbinic literature there are a number of works, mainly by the Rishonim, that were composed to determine which commandments belong in this enumeration.

The following are excerpts from a governmental manual on elder abuse:

What is Elder Abuse?

"Elder Abuse" refers to several different kinds of abuse — physical, financial, and neglect — committed against an older person. Depending on the particular law, an "elder person" is either a person who is 60 years and older or 65 years and older.

Some different types of abuse include:

Physical Abuse:

Hitting, slugging, pinching, slapping, or other acts resulting in injuries, including bruises, burns, broken bones or pain. Physical abuse also includes sexual abuse.

Neglect:

The failure of a person, such as a caregiver or a guardian, to make sure your basic needs are taken care of to the point that you are harmed. Your basic needs include:

Clean clothes and a clean bed
Adequate food
Medical care
Safe Place to live
Visits by family, friends or caregiver

Financial Abuse:

Taking or using your money, property or personal information without your consent for another person's gain. Examples of financial abuse include:

Using your name, birth date and social security number to obtain credit cards, or financial loans in your name and ruining your credit.

Telemarketers calling you to get your money or sell you bad home repair or product.

A guardian or agent who is using your money for their own needs rather than your needs.

Some Common Concerns of Elder Abuse Victims:

I don't want to get my family member in trouble.

It is my fault that my son or daughter behaves like this.

I don't want to go to a Nursing Home.

I don't want my friends and family to know what happened.

Can't we just drop it? I don't want to bother anyone else. Just let me be.

I can't hear what you are saying and won't be able to hear what the judge says.

I have no way of getting there. My granddaughter was my only source of transportation.

My husband and I have been married for more that fifty years. I cannot leave him now.

Question: "How do we honor an abusive parent?"[23]

Answer: One of the thorniest questions that a Christian may be asked or have to face up to himself is how to honor an abusive parent as required by God in the fifth of the Ten Commandments (Exodus 20:12). It would be so much easier if God had asked only that we honor our parents if they are good, kind and loving to us, but unfortunately this commandment says honor your father and mother, period. There are many, many hurt and damaged people who find this nearly impossible to obey.

The word 'abuse' is wide-ranging in its definition. A child can be brought up well clothed and fed with all its needs supplied except the all-important need for love and approval. No physical harm is ever done to him, and yet as each year goes by his spirit shrivels up inside him more and more as a plant will shrivel without sunlight, desperate for the smallest demonstration of affection, until he becomes a seemingly normal adult, yet is crippled inside by the indifference of his parents.

Then again, a child's spirit may be broken at an early age, even though he suffers no physical abuse, by being constantly told that he is useless and a waste of space who will never be good for anything. Anything he attempts is sneered at until he gives up trying to do anything at all. Because children naturally believe what their parents say about them when they are very young, the child who suffers this treatment will gradually withdraw into himself, retiring behind an invisible wall and simply existing rather than living. All these are the children who grow up into people who have never suffered physically at the hands of their parents but nevertheless have become crippled in their spirits, find it difficult to make friends, and are unable to relate normally to other adults.

What I have described above are the more subtle forms of child abuse, and moving on from this there is, of course, the obvious kind; the child who is neglected, kicked and beaten and worse still, sexually abused. So now comes the big question: how to obey God's commandment to honor parents who behave with such cruelty to their own children.

The first thing we have to remember is that God is our loving Heavenly Father who does not just slap down a rule and sit back waiting for us to disobey it. His rules and precepts are there for one reason only - our ultimate good. If we truly desire to obey Him no matter how impossible it seems, He is willing and anxious to help us find the way. First and foremost, of course, we must develop a loving, trusting relationship with our Heavenly Father which may be extremely difficult for those who have never known what it is to love and trust. I would say to those in this position to just take one small step - say to God in your heart 'I want to learn to love and trust you - please help me'. He is the only one who can change emotions and attitudes and mend damaged relationships and broken hearts (Luke 4:18).

Once this relationship with Him is established we can confidently go to

Him and pour out our problems to Him, knowing that He will hear and answer (1John 5:14-15). I can say with absolute certainty that it will not be long before any child of God willing to trust Him in this way will begin to sense the Holy Spirit at work on his heart. He will take the heart that has been turned to stone by the abusive childhood he has suffered and begin His wonderful saving work of turning that heart into one of flesh and feeling (Ezekiel 35:26).

The <u>next step</u> is to be willing to forgive. This again will seem to be utterly impossible, especially for those who have suffered the worse kind of abuse, but with God ALL things are possible (Mark 10:27). Bitterness will have sunk into the souls of these tragic victims like iron, yet there is nothing the Holy Spirit cannot soften if the person concerned is willing. All that is necessary is to daily bring the situation before the Father of all mercies and talk to Him about how impossible it is that such wicked behavior, particularly from parents that were entrusted to love and nurture us as children, could ever be forgiven.

There is no need to be afraid to admit a total inability to forgive to the

Father ... but a Father who has only a heart full of overwhelming love, compassion, mercy and a desire to help.

Once the Holy Spirit has gently and tenderly begun His healing work on us we will find ourselves looking at our parents in a different light. ... God requires that we go to Him for help to forgive so that (a) these parents will be released

from our judgment ...and (b) so that our own souls and spirits will not become gradually poisoned and twisted by the root of bitterness that no-forgiveness produces, which will sink itself deeper and deeper into our hearts and minds as time goes on.

I have often heard quite incredible testimonies from those who suffered unbelievable cruelty and lack of love at their parents' hands, and yet having learned to depend utterly on the mercy and strength of Almighty God, they have gradually found healing for their hearts and spirits and forgiveness. If you have ever suffered in this way as a child, then I pray that this may also be the ending to your story. Ephesians 6:2-3 tells us, "Honor your father and mother" - which is the first commandment with a promise - "that it may go well with you and that you may enjoy long life on the earth."[1]

SomeVerses on Death:
Some additional verses from the Bible on death:

1 Thessalonians 4:13-18
4:13

But I do not want you to be ignorant, brethren, concerning those who have fallen asleep, lest you sorrow as others who have no hope.

4:14

For if we believe that Jesus died and rose again, even so God will bring with Him those who sleep in Jesus.

4:15

For this we say to you by the word of the Lord, that we who are alive and remain until the coming of the Lord will by no means precede those who are asleep.

4:16

For the Lord He will descend from heaven with a shout, with the voice of an archangel, and with the trumpet of God. And the dead in Christ will rise first.

4:17

Then we who are alive and remain shall be caught up together with them in the clouds to meet the Lord in the air. And thus we shall always be with the Lord.

4:18

Therefore comfort one another with these words

Romans 14:8
14:8

If we live, we live to the Lord; and if we die, we die to the Lord. So, whether we live or die, we belong to the Lord.

Hebrews 2:14-15
2:14

Inasmuch then as the children have partaken of flesh and blood, He Himself likewise shared in the same, that through death He might destroy him who had the power of death, that is, the devil,
2:15

And release those who through fear of death were all their lifetime subject to bondage.

John 11:25-26
11:25

Jesus said to her, "I am the resurrection and the life. He who believes in me will live, even though he dies;
11:26

And whoever lives and believes in me will never die. Do you believe this?"

1 John 3:16
3:16

This is how we know what love is: Jesus Christ laid down his life for us. And we ought to lay down our lives for our brothers

James 4:13-14
4:13

Now listen, you who say, "Today or tomorrow we will go to this or that city, spend a year there, carry on business and make money."

4:14

Why, you do not even know what will happen tomorrow. What is your life? You are a mist that appears for a little while and then vanishes.

Matthew 10:28
10:28

Do not be afraid of those who kill the body but cannot kill the soul. Rather, be afraid of the One who can destroy both soul and body in hell.

2 Corinthians 5:1
5:1

Now we know that if the earthly tent we live in is destroyed, we have a building from God, an eternal house in heaven, not built by human hands.

Romans 8:38-39
8:38

For I am persuaded that neither death nor life, nor angels nor principalities nor powers, nor things present nor things to come,

8:39

Nor height nor depth, nor any other created thing, shall be able to separate us from the love of God which is in Christ Jesus our Lord.

Matthew 24:44
24:44

Therefore you also be ready, for the Son of Man is coming at an hour you do not expect.

Revelation 2:10
2:10

Do not fear any of those things which you are about to suffer. Indeed, the devil is about to throw some of you into prison, that you may be tested, and you will have tribulation ten days. Be faithful until death, and I will give you the crown of life.

Luke 9:24
9:24

For whoever desires to save his life will lose it, but whoever loses his life for My sake will save it.

1 Corinthians 15:54-57
15:54

So when this corruptible has put on incorruption, and this mortal has put on immortality, then shall be brought to pass the saying that is written: "Death is swallowed up in 15:55

"O Death, where is your sting? O Hades, where is your victory?" victory."

15:56

The sting of death is sin, and the strength of sin is the law

15:57

But thanks be to God, who gives us the victory through our Lord Jesus Christ.

John 11:25
11:25

Jesus said to her, "I am the resurrection and the life. He who believes in Me, though he may die, he shall live.

Job 30:23

30:23 For I know that You will bring me to death, And to the house appointed for all living.

Numbers 23:10b

23:10b Let me die the death of the righteous, and let my end be like His!

Psalms 49:10
49:10

For He sees wise men die; likewise the fool and the senseless person perish, and leave their wealth to others.

Romans 6:23

6:23 For the wages of sin is death, but the gift of God is eternal life in Christ Jesus our Lord.

Ecc 7:2

7:2 Better to go to the house of mourning than to go to the house of feasting, For that is the end of all men; And the living will take it to heart.

HONORING YOUR FATHER AND MOTHER

The following are three examples of family issues. There is no particular pattern; they are just representative of problems in our society. All authors will be anonymous for obvious reasons. Though there were many more examples, the author chose to use only three.

Example 1: *A family with eight children and many assets*

Phil was the oldest of eight children raised by parents who experienced the Great Depression and World War II. His parents were deeply committed to one another and their lives centered on family and friends. Phil had a typical baby boomer childhood in a small southern town. During his teenage years, he struggled in his relationship with his father, who, like most men of that era, used criticism and suggestions for improvement to motivate.

While Phil was away at college, he committed his life to Christ and began to grow in his new faith. He was encouraged to think Biblically about relationships, including those with his family. He realized his parents and family were perfectly selected for him by God. He wrestled with his obligation to honor his parents and began to develop personal convictions from the Scriptures about what that should look like. After some earlier false starts, he respectfully shared his faith with both his father and mother with no comments about the mainline church he had grown up in. He decided it wasn't honoring to force discussions on "deep" issues with his father since they made his father uncomfortable. He did not go back to his father and "clear the air" about things that had happened during his childhood, realizing that his father had done the best he could and God wanted that to be his experience. Phil was able to thank God for his parents and his family.

In his 30s, Phil joined his father in business, something that would have been unimaginable earlier in his life. His father retired for health reasons at 65 and asked Phil to take over the business. As the company grew, Phil found a way to work well with his father until his death. He finally stopped trying to manipulate his parents to get them to make wise choices and just gave advice or help when asked.

After his father's death, Phil spent a year as the primary person helping his mother cope with the business she now owned, a lot of real estate debt, and poorly-thought-through estate plans for dividing assets among eight children. After 18 months, he offered to buy the business from the family. They struggled through that emotional transaction while his mother received conflicting advice from various siblings. On top of that, the division of assets became problematic as the real estate, given to his sisters, and the business, given to the brothers, went in opposite directions from a value standpoint. The boys decided to even the values up by gifting assets to their sisters.

Several years after completing the purchase of the family business, there were accusations by at least one sibling suggesting Phil had taken advantage of his mother. Phil offered to give his mother the stock he had bought from her back at no charge, with the condition that he would leave the business if she felt he had inappropriately pressured her to sell or if she felt the price had not been fair. She declined the offer and relied heavily on Phil's help and advice in her last years.

At his mother's death, Phil suggested to his brothers and sisters (who had all become Christians) they consider the ongoing obligation to honor their parents even after their death by preserving their own relationships and not fighting over assets. All eight children agreed to a set of mutual convictions in handling the estate before they got into any of the details. The mutual agreement, signed by all children, included items such as:

- Their relationships with one another were more important that the "stuff";

- They would seek consensus in the division of property, but would follow majority rule;
- They would be an example of unity to the community to honor God and their parents; and
- No one would walk away from the process.

Living up to these convictions proved hard as their parents were not there to witness or referee disputes. Natural competition, emotions, long-term resentments and past offenses came to the surface. It got very sticky and emotional at times. Phil personally struggled against his tendency to justify his own rightness (which typically went in the direction of his own personal best interests). He had to work hard to go through the process with an open hand and not care how it came out.

After a number of awkward meetings, a few short-term blow-ups, and frayed emotions, the family got through it and stayed together. Phil developed the conviction that to maintain peace between his brothers and sisters probably meant not putting them in certain, unhealthy situations as a group. Getting together to "clear the air" of old hurts was definitely counter-productive. He went to each of his brothers and sisters individually to ask if there were any past offenses of his they wanted to discuss and then ask them for forgiveness. He did not allow them to decide any appropriate corrective action, but sought outside counsel for wisdom and direction on any action he should take.

Handling Phil's aging in-laws was easier. When Phil's mother-in-law could no longer live alone, he and his wife prayerfully invited her to live with them for the last years of her life. They did not ask for any help from her brothers. His mother-in-law died in their home at the age of 92. Phil helped his wife as she had helped him. They were able to walk through the division of her mother's assets with her two brothers without incident.

Example 2: *A son reaches back to his Dad who had left the family years earlier. Excerpts from the eulogy given by the Son.*

George Carson Bailey Eulogy
December 13, 2000
By his Son

Introduction

Dad was born November 29, 1935 in Salyersville, Kentucky. He was delivered by Dr. Conley, relative to Dad's mother who was a Conley. Not only did we have a doctor in the family, but a preacher. Wallace Bailey was the pastor of the Baptist church in Salyersville, Ala. around 1800. The Baileys and Conleys were well known families in the community. In fact, they celebrated the Baileys on Founders Day 1986 in the small community of Salyersville.

Personality
Dad was a loner, a gypsy, stubborn, headstrong; he spoke his mind, was independent, unconventional and a strange mixture of a liberal conservative. I love my Dad for many reasons one of which he was himself. You never wondered what Dad meant; some times you wished he were a little more tactful in his delivery and tone. He was somewhat rough on the outside but warm on the inside.

Military
Dad badly wanted to leave his small, rural roots. He struck out on his own early in life by joining the army. He served his country well for two years during the Korean conflict. He stayed stateside and even received a medal of conduct when Uncle Sam discharged him.

Marriage/Divorce

Part of his military travels brought him towards Huntsville, Alabama, where Mother had moved from Rockledge, Al. I was soon born in 1960 and my brother Mitch three years later in 1963. Sadly, Dad and Mother's marriage came to an abrupt end by divorce in 1965. Even as a five year old I was angry, hurt and disillusioned.

My Character Building

Looking back, the challenges of the family's divorce experience brought us closer to each other and to God. I learned forgiveness, hard work, discipline, teamwork and business savvy. Mostly, through this process, I found God through Jesus Christ.

Growing up as a child, Mitch and I would travel a couple a weeks a year to visit Dad and his new wife Pat in Panama City, Florida. It was exciting going to places like Panama City, fishing and catching our limit since the "blues" were "running". These were great memories.

My conversion

When I became a Christian in the spring of 1979, I wanted to express my newfound faith to those whom I loved and respected. Some were elated, others unsure and a few thought I was off my rocker. Dad was in the third group. His response was, "son, those church people have brain washed you." He said, "I have my own way of thinking; preachers used to come over to our house and preach to me, so don't preach to me".

Relationship Building

As providence would have it, I attended Southwestern Seminary in Fort Worth from 1982-85, the same time Dad worked for General Dynamics which was also in Ft. Worth. Rita, my wife, Rebekah (8 months old and the only grandchild) and I would go by for regular visits to see Dad and Pat. Even though these visits were hard, I felt Dad and I grow much closer during this time. It was eerie how much I saw myself in him and how much he saw himself in me. Though we didn't always agree, we respected and loved each other.

Health Decline

As time passed, I went to work in churches and Dad and Pat did their thing. At best Dad maintained his health; however in 1989 he had open-heart surgery at 53. I flew into Cedar Rapids, Iowa to be with him and Pat. I prayed for him before he went in and wept for him when he came out of surgery. I hurt for him as he lay there. The surgery was inevitable; however his heart was not to be the same ever again.

The dysfunctional heartbeat needed correction. Doctors attempted to help with a new still-being-tested defibulator, which malfunctioned and caused Dad more problems. After this, it was a downward spiral.

A Fighter

Dad was also a fighter. The reason he survived a heart attack at age 33 was his ability to persevere, move forward, and never give up. Life to Dad was a daily adventure. He knew he was living on borrowed time as early as age 40. He was extremely conscious that everyday was a gift from God. Maybe that's why he was so mature, focused and sometimes demanding.

A Giver

Dad was a Shiner; he gave to support the local effort to help sick children. Children had a soft spot in Dad's heart. He loved his grandchildren. His mind was sharp always capturing those details that only a caring grandfather would remember. How is their school? Tell me about their basketball. Are any boys hanging around? One Christmas, Dad and Pat came to stay with us. During their stay he hired three men to build the girls a playhouse you would have thought was the Ritz Carlton. The girls still affectionate call it granddaddy's playhouse.

A Christian

The last point I want to mention is Dad's faith. Many had prayed for Dad's spiritual and physical health over the years. One of those prayer requests was for Dad to know God in a personal way through Jesus Christ. It came after one of his near death experiences. From his hospital bed, over the phone, he expressed to me that God had a purpose for him. God had allowed him to live for a reason. He believed in Christ and wanted to do his will.

Example 3: *A letter written from a father to a son explaining the need for forgiveness and an honoring relationship even though the father had divorced and remarried. This letter was never sent. It is published with the permission of the father.*

Honor Your Father and Mother

Please read the following 12 passages (from the New International Version Bible) about honoring your parents, before reading the body of the article.

Passage 1: The Ten Commandments, Exodus 20 1-17
    (1) And God spoke all these words:
   #1 (2) "I am the LORD your God, who brought you out of Egypt, out of the land of slavery. (3) You shall have no other gods before me.

#2 (4) You shall not make for yourself an idol in the form of anything in heaven above or on the earth beneath or in the waters below. (5) You shall not bow down to them or worship them; for I, the LORD your God, am a jealous God, punishing the children for the sin of the fathers to the third and fourth generation of those who hate me, (6) but showing love to a thousand generations of those who love me and keep my commandments.

#3 (7) You shall not misuse the name of the LORD your God, for the LORD will not hold anyone guiltless who misuses his name.

#4 (8) Remember the Sabbath day by keeping it holy. (9) Six days you shall labor and do all your work, (10) but the seventh day is a Sabbath to the LORD your God. On it you shall not do any work, neither you, nor your son or daughter, nor your manservant or maidservant, nor your animals, nor the alien within your gates." (11) For in six days the LORD made the heavens and the earth, the sea, and all that is in them, but he rested on the seventh day. Therefore the LORD blessed the Sabbath day and made it holy.

#5 (12) **"Honor your father and your mother, so that you may live long in the land the LORD your God is giving you.**

#6 (13) You shall not murder.

#7 (14) You shall not commit adultery.

#8 (15) You shall not steal.

#9 (16) You shall not give false testimony against your neighbor.

#10 (17) You shall not covet your neighbor's house. You shall not covet your neighbor's wife, or his manservant or maidservant, his ox or donkey, or anything that belongs to your neighbor."

Passage 2: Exodus 20:12

"Honor your father and your mother, so that you may live long in the land the LORD your God is giving you."

Passage 3: Leviticus 19:3

"Each of you must respect his mother and father, and you must observe my Sabbaths. I am the LORD your God."

Passage 4: Leviticus 20:9

"If anyone curses his father or mother, he must be put to death. He has cursed his father or mother and his blood will be on his own head."

Passage 5: Deuteronomy 5:16

"Honor your father and your mother, as the LORD your God has commanded you, so that you may live long and that it may go well with you in the land the LORD your God is giving you."

Passage 6: Deuteronomy 27:16

"Cursed is the man who dishonors his father or his mother." Then all the people shall say, "Amen!"

Passage 7: Matthew 15:4

For God said, "Honor your father and mother" and "Anyone who curses his father or mother must be put to death."

Passage 8: Matthew 19:16-19

(16) Now a man came up to Jesus and asked, "Teacher, what good thing must I do to get eternal life?" (17) "Why do you ask me about what is good?" Jesus replied. "There is only One who is good. If you want

to enter life, obey the commandments." (18) "Which ones?" the man inquired. Jesus replied, "'Do not murder, do not commit adultery, do not steal, do not give false testimony', (19) 'Honor your father and mother', and 'love your neighbor as yourself'."

Passage 9: Mark 7:8-10

(8) "You have let go of the commands of God and are holding on to the traditions of men." (9) And he said to them: "You have a fine way of setting aside the commands of God in order to observe your own traditions! (10) For Moses said, 'Honor your father and your mother', and, 'Anyone who curses his father or mother must be put to death'.

Passage 10: Mark 10:19

"You know the commandments: 'Do not murder, do not commit adultery, do not steal, do not give false testimony, do not defraud, honor your father and mother'."

Passage 11: Luke 18:20

"You know the commandments: 'Do not commit adultery, do not murder, do not steal, do not give false testimony, honor your father and mother'."

Passage 12: Ephesians 6:1-3

(1) Children, obey your parents in the Lord, for this is right. (2) "Honor your father and mother"—which is the first commandment with a promise— (3) "that it may go well with you and that you may enjoy long life on the earth."

Observations and Applications of these Passages

Whew! When you string all of these verses together they are shocking.

A "blind spot" is an interesting thing. We all have them. Our most common experience with one is when we are driving. We look in our left mirror to see if it is clear to change lanes and there is nothing there. Yet sure enough another car is there and when we turn, they honk to warn us. We barely miss having an accident. If we have a parabolic mirror on our side mirror, we can glance in it and see the reality of the situation clearly. The car is there and we don't make the lane change.

We all have blind spots. Situations are clearly in our life and we just don't see them. Maybe we look in the side mirror briefly, but we don't see reality. The Bible is the parabolic mirror of life. When we look intently at it, it will show us when there is, in fact, a car in the other lane; we then can avoid the turn that results in an accident. The blind spot is revealed and saves us from having a "life wreck."

Every generation has blind spots. Every organization and every church has them. In fact in Revelations Jesus writes letters to the seven churches, outlining their blind spots.

Think about the passages above. The Lord starts out the Ten Commandments outlining four critical attitudes and behaviors of his people toward Him. This is square one, our conduct toward our Heavenly Father, His Only Son - our Lord and Savior and the Holy Spirit.

Then our Heavenly Father moves on to the relationship of his people to each other. The first command to each other is not in relation to murder, adultery, stealing or lying. You have often heard that God does not rank one sin above another and I suppose that is true. Nevertheless, His first shot out of the gun is not murder or adultery or lying.

We all know that murder, adultery and lying are terrible things. Lord knows we abhor those sins. Lord knows that the consequence of those sins is horrifying, debilitating and destructive. But Lord, did you really mean to put honoring, or should we say dishonoring, our parents on equal footing to murder, adultery and lying? Surely Lord, you have made a mistake here. This is probably a mix up. We maybe could understand putting it after stealing and lying, yet Lord if we were making the list we wouldn't even put it on there.

First on the list — Lord, this has to be an error! Lord, you are outlining here in the second book of the Bible, ten of the most important things you want us to remember, obey, take note of and heed. The first four are the importance of how we view and behave toward you. The next six lay out how we conduct ourselves toward each other and you start off numero uno with how we treat and view our parents? How we think and behave toward our mother and father. Could this be more important than murder, adultery and lying? Obviously it is on equal footing. Yeah, let's not put it first, even though you did, Lord. Let's just not put ourselves on too much of a guilt trip, put it on equal footing. Yes, Lord, we want to lobby you to reduce it to equality. It is too painful to put it first.

As we search, study and meditate on the Scriptures we learn how the Lord views things. Two of my observations over the years are repetition and simplicity. If the Lord says something repetitively, then its importance is magnified. If a command or point or principle is repeated three or four times, then it is important. Six, seven or eight, we need to tune up and listen. Nine, ten, eleven, whoa this must be serious. Twelve times is off the chart. This is big time! This is of gargantuan proportion!

Often in the Bible the Lord simply addresses our defaults. Often He puts things very simply. Often He gives us few instructions, lest we get confused. For example, there is only one way to Heaven – Jesus. If there were two, we would easily spend our entire life trying to make a decision which way to go. The Lord gives little instruction on marriage. Husbands love your wives! Wives respect your husbands. See how simple it is? Not long detailed lists and instructions, just a few simple words. It seems to me that our Heavenly Father does this because he knows our flesh, our behavior and our attitudes inside and out. He knows what we "default" to. Like on our computer, when it gets out-of-sorts or off-track, we hit the default button and, wham, it goes back to its original state.

Our flesh is like that. When we get out-of-sorts or off-track, we hit the button and, boom, our default sets in. Yes, just like a computer, we default to the parameters and performance that the programmer originally intended. Sadly the programmer of the flesh is a hacker. He is a virus spreader. His goal is to destroy the machine. Render it unusable. Take control of it and make it a slave to his use. He is our enemy, a terrorist. He has a name: Satan, the devil, the enemy, the deceiver. He seeks to destroy our life. Our flesh default as husbands is to not love our wives, as wives to not respect our husbands, and as children to not honor our parents.

Could it be that in the last 50 years a massive blind spot in America, in our churches and families, has been the first commandment of our behavior and attitudes toward our parents? Could we have totally missed this one? Could we have glanced in the mirror and not seen it? Yet it is right next to us. Could we be so comfortable with the status quo that we whiffed this one?

I think so. A French philosopher, Alex DeTouqville, observed in the early 1900s that America was different from Europe in that in America, parents honor their children versus children honoring their parents. He would be shocked to see how we do it today. Don't get me wrong, children are very, very important. They are the future. They are to be taught and loved and encouraged. None of us wants our kids to be murderers, adulterers, liars and thieves. Our Sunday schools, Christian schools, and vacation Bible classes clearly take a stand as to the terrible nature of these sins. Yet there is little to no instruction in the church, school or home on the equal importance of honoring your parents. Maybe we are embarrassed to ask for that from our children. Culturally in the United States today everything is about the "children", not about us as parents. We are to dedicate our life to them. We serve them. Our parents' goal was to "never be a burden to their children". With this attitude and umbrella over our relationship to our children we have missed "numero uno". We have missed the significant importance of honoring our parents. We have missed the scary consequences of dishonoring our parents.

Yes, DISHONORING OUR PARENTS. You might say, "I don't dishonor my parents." Yet, neutrality is not enough! The lack of honoring is dishonoring! The Scripture is clear. We must honor our parents if it is to go well for us! We must have a proactive lifestyle of honoring our parents. The absence of it is dishonoring!

In the church today we gloss over this critical commandment. In approximately 1,500 Sundays these past 30 years that I have actively pursued my faith in church, I have never once heard a sermon on the staggering importance of honoring my parents. Sermon after sermon has been preached on parenting, on marriage, on being a good father or husband or wife or mother, but never on the importance of a lifestyle of HONORING MY PARENTS.

Do you see the importance of all of this? How can we have a healthy relationship with our Heavenly Father, whom we can't see, if we don't honor our earthly father or mother, whom we can see? How can we honor our Heavenly Father if we dishonor our mother and father? Remember, neutrality is not an option. The lack of honor is dishonoring!

But you say, "My situation is different!" "My parents were not very nice." "My mother hurt my feelings back when I was 16 and I can't get over that." "You see my dad was an angry man." "My dad or mother committed adultery." "My mother was a drinker." "My dad was all work, no play." "My parents did not come to my activities." "My parents wouldn't pay my way to college." "My parents never gave me encouragement." "My parents wouldn't financially support me like other kids." "My parents talked down to me." "My parents were never there for me." "My parents argued all the time." "My parents divorced." "My parents were…" on and on and on!

"Yeah Lord, you just don't know what I have been through. If you had only known my parents, then you wouldn't have even put that "Honor Your Mother and Father" stuff on the list. Yeah Lord, if you only knew my pain. Lord, I didn't get a fair shake when you handed out parents. Yeah Lord, you made a mistake when you gave me my parents. How could you be so unfair? How dare you ask me to honor the pitiful excuse of parents you gave me! Surely you didn't mean it, Lord, when you commanded me to honor these parents!

But you know Lord, I have an excuse. I t is their fault. That's right, they made me do it. My parents are the problem, not me. I really wanted to honor my parents but they are so bad. Lord, I have a pass. How could anyone honor parents like this? Lord, you have no idea what it is like to have a parent like mine. This isn't fair! Most of my friends got a better deal than me. Why, if I had parents like them, this would be much easier.

Yeah Lord, it is kind of your fault too. You gave me these imperfect sinful excuses of a mother or father. You say you knitted me in my mother's womb. You say I am the seed of my father. But how can that be? You say you knew me before I was born, so how could you have given me these guys? Lord, it was a mistake. I needed you to give me perfect parents before I can do this "Honoring" thing. Lord, I want my parents to be perfect, just like me. Then Lord, if they were perfect, I could honor them. And then Lord, if I could be perfect, then maybe you could let me into your heaven. Then you could give me salvation. Then there would be no need to forgive my sins."

Oops! Now this is beginning to hurt. For you see there is no such thing as a perfect parent. Could this be the heart of this issue? Could this be one of the reasons that this is the first commandment as to our relations with others?

You see it would seem easy to honor an honorable parent. Although in reality, most do a poor job of honoring an honorable parent. Sadly, we are all so self-centered that we rarely get around to it. But then give us the excuse of our parent being dishonorable, an imperfect performer. Man, does this ever give me an out. Lord, this gives me a pass. Lord, you made a mistake here. You didn't mean it when you told me to honor my parents.

Or maybe this is the rub! Maybe this is the acid test! Can I honor the position of my parents in spite of their imperfect performance? Can I honor the Lord, my God, by obeying the first of his commandments in relation to my behavior to others?

Could this be the big blind spot of our generation? Could Satan be having a field day with our missing this unbelievably important command? The answer is obvious.

We have our whole society working to hinder this command. We have Social Security, Medicare and Medicaid, so the government has responsibility to take care of our parents, not us. We have parents who would do anything to "not to be a burden to their children". However, it seems to me that our children's taking care of us is God's plan from the get-go. We have parents scrimping and saving for their retirement in order that they won't need a dime from their kids. We have parents doing everything they can possibly do for their children, selfishly hoping at the end of the day those same children would honor them by saying, "Hey, thanks for being such great parents." Yet when the day is over most of our children say, "What are you going to do for me next?"

What do we do about this? Where do we start?

Parents of young children need to make a priority of demonstrating how adults continue to honor their parents. If they ever hope to see their children obey the 5th Commandment, this is a good place to start. I f they ever hope to see their children receive the promised blessing of this commandment; they must up-tick their performance as adult children to their parents.

Parents must make it a major priority to teach their children to respect them and honor them, to educate their children on how important this is to God. How, if the Scriptures are true (and we believe they are), children must get this right if they are ever to truly succeed in life. You frequently hear parents say, "I just want my kids to be happy." If we really mean this, then we must take this commandment at face value. We must take its twelve references as a major ingredient as stated in Ephesians 6:3, "that it may go well and that you may enjoy a long life."

You see the antithesis of this is that it will not go well for us, or our children, if we miss the importance of this commandment. As a matter of fact, the Word of God is tougher than that. In America today we seem to only look at this as a blessing. If you honor your parents it will go well for you is the primary thought. Oh, this is a sweet verse with a blessing. Yet if you survey the twelve verses it is not a pretty picture. Half of the tenor is that (Deut. 27:16) "Cursed is the man who dishonors his father or his mother." Jesus even repeats this in Mark 7:8-10 and Luke 18. The inference in the Old and New Testament is that anyone who dishonors or curses his father or mother is worthy of death.

Do you see both sides of this coin? If you honor your father and mother, there is a wonderful blessing. If you dishonor or curse your mother or father, you are worthy of death!

Back to how do we do this. We do it a step at a time.

If your parents are alive you start today. It isn't hard. It is a bunch of little things. For example, phone your parents every week or two. Tell them thanks for all they have done for you. Tell them you love them. Remember something special they said or did and relate it to them.

Write your parents a love letter once a year. Tell them how much you love them, how much you appreciate how hard it was to be a parent and all they did for you. Thank them for all the meals, clothes washed, diapers changed, messes cleaned up, and on and on.

Call your Mother and Dad the first thing when you wake up on your birthday and especially thank your Mother for doing all the work on that day. Thank them for naming you and all the effort to bring you into this world. You just came out crying and demanding a meal (kept on doing that for years)! I always thought we had birthdays backwards in America. We should throw a party for our parents, not they throw one for us.

If your parents are deceased and you haven't honored them as you should, it is not too late. Write them a letter thanking them for all they did. Tell them you love them. Ask forgiveness for dishonoring them. Then put it in a drawer. The Lord heard it and you heard it. It will bring healing and joy.

By the way, if you are married, you now have four parents. It won't suffice to ignore your mother and father in-law or to relegate that responsibility to your spouse. If you and your husband have become one flesh, then you now have two sets of parents. Both husband and wife need to honor the other's parents as well as their own.

Forgiveness is a wonderful gift from the Lord. I especially appreciate it in light of the daily repetitive sins for which Jesus forgives me. Many of us need to ask one or both of our parents for forgiveness. Sometimes it is for forgiveness for our rude or self-centered behavior and attitudes. Sometimes it is for forgiveness for our neutrality in honoring them. If we do ask our parents for forgiveness it needs to be without expecting results or response on their part. If we can go to them humbly and without excuse, it gives the opportunity for healing. We can say, "Mother forgive me for the times I have lashed out to you in anger. I love you. I want to honor you as the mother that God gave me. Will you forgive me?" Worst case is that nothing happens. Best case is that you repair a bridge in one of the most important relationships you will ever have. Your parents' response is their issue; your humility and obedience is a love offering to the Lord and will please Him.

You might say again, "You just don't know my dad or my mother." But I say, even the worst parent was made in the image of God and has some redeeming qualities. The God of all creation assigned these parents to you! Are you going to show God he is wrong, that He made a mistake? Are you going to focus on the negative or the positive? Can you sit down and list the positive traits and honor them for those traits even when they are few? Grace is not, "getting what you deserve" but "getting what you don't deserve." We want grace. Can we give it? Even the worst parent, according to our God, is deserving of honor! It is interesting over the years to observe children whose fathers went to prison or whose mothers were horrible performers and yet they honored or loved them. Then you can observe children who have no regard for relatively good performing parents. The high road is to honor your parents in either case. It is a no-lose situation. This is an equal opportunity for all children. Those with good, marginal or bad parents are blessed by obeying the 5th Commandment!

Do you see it? This is the 5th Commandment, not the 5th Option. We have to choose to obey or not obey. No choice is a choice to disobey or a choice to dishonor.

Do you see it? Your parents spend 16-21 years taking care of you and you spend the next 45 to 50 years thanking them and honoring them and maybe even taking care of them. You don't have to grovel. Just a phone call here, a note there, a note from the grandkids, a picture, a post card, a Christmas card, an Easter card, birthday, Father's Day, Mother's Day, Thanksgiving... It is not rocket science. Take them out to dinner or have them over for dinner. It doesn't take a lot. It would only cost a little, yet mean so much: a small investment that yields great dividend.

Do you see what a blessing this would be to good parents, marginal parents and bad parents? Do you see how it could positively impact a hardened, grouchy old parent? Do you see how it could change your attitude, your perspective? Do you see how it could impact your children to see how and why you honor your parents, so that when your children become adults, they too will know how to obey this command and reap its blessings?

From a selfish standpoint you can't lose if you do this. You can't win if you don't. Assume you will see no change in your parents' attitude, behavior or performance. The command is not contingent upon their response. It is your obedience that is important here.

You see, as usual with the Lord, when you obey and do what is right, you are the big winner. God loves us. He never asks us to do anything that is not for our best interest. When you start a lifestyle of honoring your parents, hard as it may be, you are blessed. Things will go well for you; you will live a long and happy life.

Now this is a formula that should sell in books and tapes. Come one, come all! Follow these simple steps and the God of Creation promises you well-being and a long life!

Today is the first day of the rest of your life. Make a commitment to honor your mother and father so that it may go well for you, your parents and your children!

Endnotes

1   Isaiah 7:14 & 40:3, Mic 5:2

2   Greek dictionary

3   Matthew 25:2

4   Pictorial Bible Dictionary, page 182

5   John 14:21

6   Ephesians 5:25

7   Proverbs 22:15

8   Luke 6:27-36

9   1 Co 3:16-17

10 Mathew 8:22

11 II Co 8:9

12 Lev 19:32

[13] Malachi 2:16

[14] *Beside Still Waters*; C.H. Spurgeon; Thomas Nelson Publishers; page 354

[15] 1 Corinthians 15:26

[16] Psalm 116:15

[17] Philippians 1:21

[18] Psalm 90:12

[19] Ezekiel 33:11

[20] Philippians 1:21

[21] 88Maimonides: *Sefer Hamitzvot* ("Book of Commandments") with a critical commentary of Nachmanides

[22] Talmud Yerusahlmi, Peah I:1

[23] Excerpts from "Got Questons.org" April, 2006

Printed in the United States
207346BV00001B/1-201/P

9 781606 472729